STONYPATH DAYS

STONYPATH DAYS

LETTERS BETWEEN IAN HAMILTON FINLAY AND STEPHEN BANN 1970–72

Edited and introduced by
Stephen Bann

WILMINGTON SQUARE BOOKS
an imprint of Bitter Lemon Press

Supported by a Publications Grant from the Paul Mellon Centre for Studies in British Art

Supported by The Henry Moore Foundation

WILMINGTON SQUARE BOOKS
An imprint of Bitter Lemon Press

First published in 2016 by
Wilmington Square Books
47 Wilmington Square
London WC1X 0ET

www.bitterlemonpress.com

A CIP record for this book is available from the British Library

ISBN 978-1-908524-720

2 4 6 8 9 7 5 3 1

Designed and typeset by Jane Havell Associates
Printed in China

CONTENTS

PREFACE

IN COMPILING this second collection of my correspondence with Ian Hamilton Finlay, I have been well aware of the different message that comes across to the reader who traces the events of the two years in question. The first collection, *Midway*, covered a period of rapid development, and often perilous innovation, in Finlay's work as a poet and artist. Between the autumn of 1964 and the autumn of 1966, he lived in three different locations. Having moved with his wife Sue from Edinburgh to the rented accommodation of Gledfield Farmhouse in the early summer of 1965, he was able to carry out his cherished plan of realising his poems in the form of constructions, and sited these new works throughout the house and its surrounding garden. But this respite was for hardly more than a year. After spending a brief interval of a few months in the cramped surroundings of a small house in Fife, the Finlays and their two children finally moved to the farm of Stonypath in the autumn of 1966.

Yet in spite of the unprecedented opportunities that arose from this newfound security of tenure, it was still an arduous task to balance the different roles that Finlay had assumed over the previous few years. After being hospitalised for a serious heart condition in the winter of 1967/68, he decided that it was necessary to relinquish his poetry magazine, *Poor. Old. Tired. Horse.*, and to confine the Wild Hawthorn Press to his own publications. He continued to develop the distinctive genre of the 'poem/print' and to publish cards and booklets. But the more ambitious schemes of involving other artists and craft specialists in collaborative projects often proved all too difficult to carry through without mishap and frustration. Opportunities did arise to exhibit his work in Scotland and in London. But, with a few exceptions, the critical response was baffled and negative.

The one area in which significant progress was being made, none the less, was in the creation of the garden at Stonypath. With the invaluable cooperation of Sue, who devised the planting schemes, Finlay began to transform the areas surrounding the farmhouse, which ranged from an overgrown Front Garden to sloping stretches of wild moorland irrigated by a precious burn. This collection borrows the title, *Stonypath Days*, from the first short film on the garden, which I arranged to be shot by James Styles in the summer of 1973. By that point, the number of visitors who flocked to Stonypath in the summer months was providing ample proof of its growing reputation. The inhibitions that still came to the fore when Finlay's work was shown in the context of a gallery installation were seemingly vanquished when his sundials and inscribed stones were observed in a natural setting. But, of course, the setting was not simply 'natural'. Finlay had devoted considerable care and attention to the question of what constituted a garden, in cultural as well as purely physical terms. In particular, he had thought deeply about the question of how a garden might be 'art', and not just in the hybrid sense of being indirectly related to the traditions of poetry, architecture and painting. I would contend that the years 1970–71 were decisive in enabling him to arrive at this realisation, and the letters that follow here illuminate some of the stages through which it was reached.

Whereas in *Midway* only Finlay's side of the correspondence could be published, in this collection my own letters to him are also included. For the foregoing period from 1964 onwards, a high proportion of the letters that Finlay wrote to me had found their way into the Special Collections of the Library of the University of Kansas – acting according to the prompt of Mike Weaver, who had initially introduced me to Finlay, I had sold them for his benefit. Though he was grateful for this financial help, Finlay certainly did not view the saleable character of his letters with complete equanimity. In 1972, he was disturbed by the fact that an old friend had made another such sale, which included confessional material from an early and very turbulent period of his life. He was also alert, as shown by one of the letters that follows, to the likelihood that unscrupulous correspondents might inveigle him into pointless and interminable exchanges with a view to capitalising on them. But for the period covered by this volume, he had determined to arrange the bulk of his correspondence specifically with a view to its being included in a public collection. The Lilly Library at the University of Indiana had agreed to purchase the material that related to his collaborative projects, and this arrangement continued over a five-year period from c. 1967 until the beginning of 1972. My own letters being part of this archive, I have been able to intersperse them here with the Finlay letters that remain in my own possession. The two years 1970 and 1971 were periods of incessant activity in both of our lives, and this exchange of letters bears witness to their intensity.

*

I am pleased to acknowledge the support of Susan Swan, who warmly welcomed the publication of the *Midway* collection. I hope that she will recover here some vivid memories of the great garden that she helped to create.

I am much indebted to the thoughtful responses of Pia Simig, who gave me permission to publish these letters on behalf of the Estate of Ian Hamilton Finlay, and encouraged me in particular to incorporate my own side of the correspondence. It is also a pleasure to place on record the generous cooperation of the staff of the Lilly Library, University of Indiana, which holds such an extensive archive that bears on Finlay's early work. The Lilly provided copies of my own letters, after my initial visit to the library in 2009. I am indeed grateful to Zachary Downey who at a late stage helped me to locate a couple of them that had gone astray.

Although I am no longer a trustee of Little Sparta, I am delighted to record my appreciation of the success of the Trust in ensuring that the garden continues to flourish, and hope that my own efforts will continue to contribute to this noble end. I should mention in particular the dedication of the Chairman of Trustees, Magnus Linklater, and the invaluable research that is now being undertaken by Patrick Eyres, with regard to the objects in the garden, and Ian Kennedy, with reference to Finlay's library. George Gilliland's attention to the maintenance of Little Sparta, both respectful and creative, also deserves a mention here.

These letters benefit immeasurably from being juxtaposed with a number of slides taken at the time by Tony Grist, who accompanied me on my visits to Stonypath in 1971 and 1972 and has generously put them at my disposal. Virtually all the images taken by professional photographers throughout this period are in black-and-white. These so far unpublished colour prints have a vividness and, on occasions, a welcome informality that accords well with the tone of our exchanges.

John Nicoll has once again merited my gratitude by agreeing to publish this sequel to the *Midway* collection, which benefits from the same high standards of design and production as its predecessor.

NOTE TO THE READER

Virtually all the letters that are published here are transcribed, as nearly as possible, in their original form. Brief messages and notes sent to me over the same period, usually consisting of a single sheet of paper or a postcard with a simple greeting, have been omitted from the correspondence, as have occasional letters from third parties or newspaper cuttings sent as enclosures. Square brackets are used throughout the text to indicate my editorial interventions. It should however be noted that Finlay himself often used brackets (here shown as round), for example to enclose the word 'sic'.

On occasions, Finlay would also question (with good reason) his first attempt at spelling a word, but such 'mistakes' have been retained, being often inseparable from the ingenious word-play that is a recurring feature of the letters. Brief annotations to the text of the letters, marked by Finlay with asterisks, are incorporated with their asterisks into the text. Care has been taken to retain the spontaneity of the writing by retaining his frequent use of ellipses of different lengths (two, three, four or more periods) to indicate variable breaks in continuity. Divisions between paragraphs are also sometimes accentuated by the insertion of a single period.

The Finlay letters transcribed here are drawn almost exclusively from typewritten scripts. My own letters, by contrast, were almost exclusively handwritten. Both included occasional drawings which have been reproduced here at the appropriate place in the text. Whereas a certain proportion of the earlier letters from Finlay that were published in *Midway* were difficult to date, and required confirmation through a post-mark, the correspondence on both sides that is published here is almost invariably dated at the head of each letter. All letters from Finlay are addressed from 'Stonypath'. The majority of my letters, which are sent from my home address, are headed 'Canterbury', but full details are provided for those sent from other locations.

The two 'Lists of Works' that are appended towards the end of this volume incorporate page references to any letters in which a particular art work is noted and discussed. This makes it possible to be precise about the point at which such works had been installed in the garden, and indeed to track the early development of an idea or project that would later bear fruit in a work. For instance, the genesis of the Canterbury Sundial, which was finally installed on the site of the University of Kent at the end of 1972, can be traced here through a long series of discussions and design stages which had achieved a final resolution by January of the same year.

STEPHEN BANN
2016

INTRODUCTION

THE OPENING OF THE DECADE of the 1970s presaged a new phase in Ian Hamilton Finlay's creative life as an artist. In respect of his poem/prints, the genre that he had begun to develop in the mid-1960s, there were as many new works published in 1970/71 as in the entire preceding period. A similar comparison involving his production of cards and folding cards reveals that these two years alone saw an increase of roughly a third upon the number published in the earlier years. But this bare statistical record of publications tells us little about the more fundamental change that was taking place in his manner of working. The letters from 1964 to 1969 that have already been published in my *Midway* collection record, by and large, a tantalising gap between his aims and his achievements. He usually succeeded in assuring, though with a fair measure of difficulty, the adequate visual presentation of his concrete poems. But the urge to embody his poetry in a material form, whether sand-blasted on glass or (as ultimately became the case) inscribed on stone, involved close collaboration with a wide variety of craftsmen and design studios. In the worst case, these ventures only managed to achieve dubious results at considerable expense. Even the more successful collaborations could rarely be relied upon for any assurance of continuity. The lack of any confidence of being able to produce his work cooperatively, and to an agreed schedule, sometimes drove Finlay to despair.

In the light of this dilemma, the appearance of the names of both Michael Harvey and Ron Costley in the correspondence of 1970–71 sends a welcome signal. Both these outstanding practitioners of the art of lettering continued to work with Finlay over many years, and throughout the period when his preferred medium was developing from Bauhaus-inspired typography to Roman-style epigraphy and graceful italic writing. They soon set their stamp upon many of his most characteristic works. Of course, the process of collaboration did not always run smoothly, even with such highly competent and professional operators. Harvey lived and worked in Bridport, on the coast of Dorset, and so at a lengthy car journey away from the Pentland Hills. His genuine enthusiasm for the possibilities of working with Finlay was made clear to me from the start.[1] But the specific financial basis upon which his contributions were to be estimated caused a certain friction in passing, doubtless because the Finlays were undergoing a serious financial crisis at the time.[2]

Harvey's collaboration indeed proved crucial in ensuring the successful management of two major projects, the first of which was completed for the beginning of September 1970, and the second fully designed at the outset of 1972, for delivery and installation before the end of that year. Both of > pls. 2, 3 these projects were for sundials, the genre that Finlay had begun to develop in some of his earliest garden installations at Stonypath. The first of the two, which incorporated the poem *Azure & Son*, was the result of a surprise commission by the Provost of Biggar, a market town just a few miles away from Stonypath, and was promoted as a public work to commemorate European Conservation Year 1970. In this particular case, Harvey worked to an accelerated timetable, since there was barely a month to go between the Provost's initial proposal and the date that had already been designated for the ceremonial opening. In the case of the second sundial, 'Land/Sea', which was commissioned for the grounds of the University of Kent at Canterbury, the process proved rather more leisurely. I myself was responsible for proposing the commission, in my capacity as Chairman of the Senate Exhibitions Committee of this new university. The prime site in the middle of the campus that was eventually selected had the advantage of a far-away view of the towers of Richborough Power Station on the very edge of the Kent coastline.[3] Negotiations on the subject of the work's concrete base and surrounding paving dragged on quite slowly, though amicably, with the University Architect and the University Surveyor over a period of several months. The agreed choice of the design for the sundial itself marks the end-point of this volume of correspondence. Harvey advocated the polished treatment of the green slate slab in discussion with Finlay and myself, and was directly responsible for carving the dial and its inscription.

These two commissioned sundials were, respectively, Finlay's first public work to be installed in Scotland, and his first to be installed anywhere in the world outside Scotland. As such, they could be said to look backward, to the period of the mid-Sixties when he first had the intuition that his poems might

1. On 22 September 1971, Michael Harvey wrote to me: 'Thank you very much for your letter and for the nice things you say about my collaboration with Ian. Really, I am delighted to work with him and look upon it as an honour as well as a pleasure'.

2. See letter of 24 September 1971 (p. 157).

3. This power station has now been demolished. The sundial itself has been renovated and moved a few yards from the main pathway to a more secure site, while keeping the right orientation to the sun.

ultimately achieve a public and permanent expression, and forward to the long sequence of public projects that would be completed over the next three decades.[4] Yet this landmark in his career pales in significance when set beside the most significant and forward-looking development that was taking place in Finlay's art over the initial years of the 1970s. This was the accelerated movement towards maturity, and in certain respects the new orientation, of his concept of Stonypath as a garden.

In the period that had elapsed since their arrival at the farm of Stonypath in the autumn of 1966, Ian and Sue Finlay had worked unremittingly to transform their immediate environment.[5] While Sue chose and introduced plants, shrubs and trees, Ian began to engineer a sequence of ponds, channelling the water of the small burn that traversed the property. The most dramatic and definitive episode in this process of development would come in July 1971 when bulldozers were brought in to excavate the site of the future Lochan Eck, prompting Finlay to a Yeatsian exclamation: 'All is Changed, Utterly Changed, since I last wrote'.[6] By this stage, one could say, the garden had achieved an identity that required the introduction of new features, which would inevitably be of an ambitious and adventurous type. The process had in fact already started when, in May of the same year, Finlay created a small island in the previously established Top Pond, with a white bridge leading to it. In a letter of > pl. 11 24 May 1971 he revealed his intention: 'During the winter I will devise a poem for this prize site.'[7] When, in due course, Michael Harvey completed the inscription for an impressive marble structure to be placed on the > pl. 12 island, it was not so much a question of an art work being inserted in a natural setting, as of a landscape garden that had acquired an appropriately classical feature.

It is especially in the correspondence of these two important years that we can trace the emergence of the garden that would eventually, by the end of the 1970s, be named Little Sparta. This was fundamentally a matter of establishing the infrastructure of a water garden, with a succession of pools culminating in the change in scale that was made manifest with the creation of the

4. The publication *Ian Hamilton Finlay: Werke in Europa 1972–1995* (Ostfildern: Cantz, 1995) documents 95 individual objects in public places (excluding works at Little Sparta).

5. The process is clearly described, using Sue's own account, in the most recent and complete guide to the garden: Jessie Sheeler, *Little Sparta: a Guide to the Garden of Ian Hamilton Finlay* (Edinburgh: Burlinn Ltd, 2015), esp. pp. xvii–xxiv.

6. See p. 142 (letter of 20 July 1971). The reference is to W. B. Yeats's poem 'Easter 1916'.

7. See p. 126. The work eventually devised for the site employed the fishing boat name 'Silver Cloud' to stress the reciprocity between the clouds in the sky and their reflection in the pond.

largest stretch of water, named Lochan Eck after the Finlays' son. But hardly less important than this practical step was the parallel process of gaining a fuller knowledge of garden art, and the classical tradition, which was stimulated by Finlay's contemporary reading. It was at the end of June 1970 that he wrote to me with infectious enthusiasm about his recent discovery of Edward Hyams's book, *The English Garden.* Clearly this text had provided ample reassurance on a point that had been nagging him since he began to produce concrete poetry in the early 1960s. Was the new kind of work that he was doing simply a hybrid type of art, as the title of Jasia Reichardt's influential 1965 show of comparable works, *Between Poetry and Painting*, tended to suggest? This question had become even more imperative with regard to the art of gardening, which involved of necessity a range of practical as well as aesthetic decisions. Hyams, however, had resolved the issue without the slightest equivocation. A garden could indeed be a work of art. And so it ought to be.

The confirmation that he derived from Hyams led Finlay inevitably into a new engagement with the domain of culture in respect of which the garden of Stonypath still remained deficient. He recognised that there was a need to come to terms in a more consequential way with the legacy of the classical tradition. In mid-November 1970, I paid a short visit to Stonypath, and we spoke about Erwin Panofsky's essay, 'Poussin and the Elegiac tradition'. Not long afterwards, after a polite reminder, I sent him a photocopy of this evocative document of art history, which launched a train of thought that culminated in Finlay's 'Footnotes to an essay' of 1977.[8] Such a literary outcome was, however, just one aspect of a transformation in his thinking that was soon to become manifest in the planning of new features in the garden. Soon after he wrote to me of his excitement at reading Hyams's study, Finlay had remarked casually at the end of a letter: 'Did I tell you I have (meanwhile) fallen in love with battleships?' This avowal was indeed significant as it came from a poet and artist who had previously made the fishing boat, and its adventurous vicissitudes, the privileged symbol of his poetics. Fishing boats, and their symbolic representation in the form of sundial inscriptions and similar texts, did not by any means disappear from the garden overnight. But they were soon joined there by a new 'Roman Garden', in which a stone aircraft carrier played the role of a birdbath. The green slate monolith whose form derived from the conning tower of a nuclear submarine endowed the waters of Lochan Eck with an oceanic effect of scale.

8. Published in Ian Hamilton Finlay, exhibition catalogue, Serpentine Gallery, London, 1977: the 'footnotes' consisted in a series of drawings by Gary Hincks after classic landscape paintings on the theme of 'Et In Arcadia Ego', with variants devised by Finlay that installed modern weaponry in an Arcadian setting.

There are many similar tell-tale signals throughout these letters of Finlay's growing conviction of how the Stonypath garden might continue to develop, to the extent of becoming the concrete expression of his life's work. But it is worth dwelling a little, at the same time, on the fact that this is a collection of letters that comprises both sides of our correspondence. In the case of *Midway*, the previous collection of Finlay's letters to me over the period 1964–69, my own letters to him still remained for the most part inaccessible. For the period 1970–71, however, all of the letters that I sent to him were included in the Finlay archive that was sold to the Lilly Library at the time.[9]

This fortunate occurrence makes it possible to trace the exchange of ideas and perceptions that was taking place between us at the time, when I myself was beginning to write with increasing confidence on the unique character and significance of his work. Though I accepted, it would appear quite promptly and cheerfully, the task of providing texts that ranged from a few paragraphs to the proportions of a substantial essay, I was clearly doing so in the light of a spirit of mutual exchange. Few other critics managed to achieve this degree of *entente* with Finlay at the time, or at any subsequent period of his creative life. Indeed, his reputation for fearsome single-mindedness has to some extent persisted.[10] Clearly I was enthusiastic about his work, at a time when few others took the trouble to study it. But I can only assume that his pleasure in responding to my letters was, at least in part, a measure of the vastly different mode of life to which they testified. My abbreviated narratives and witty turns of phrase, taking the hint of course from his own inventive chronicles, caught his attention. The mildly scolding tone in which he comments on my taste for 'foreign' travel does not at all preclude an amused interest in such all-too-frequent excursions, from which he himself was of course still barred by his agoraphobia. I must have been conscious of appearing to be blithely self-advertising in all these accounts of my activities. But, on the other hand, the opening of the 1970s was an extraordinary period for the circulation of new ideas, and I was making the most of it.

To serve as a young lecturer in a new British university in the early 1970s was indeed an invigorating experience. Ripples from the Paris May events of

9. See also Preface, p. 8.

10. The correspondence of Finlay's friend, the American poet Jonathan Williams, is illuminating in this respect. Williams was a strong supporter of Finlay's work, and in 1971 he was planning to publish a large volume of his selected poems. None the less he assured the Scottish poet Thomas A. Clark that Finlay belonged to a class of poets who were not particularly interested in works other than their own. Finlay's letters to me, both in *Midway* and in the current publication, suggest the opposite. Williams conducted interviews with Finlay in 1972, but reported to Clark the view of Finlay that he '[did] not strike the proper posh, academic tone that S. Bann manufactures in his Kentish snuggery'. See Beinecke Library, Yale University, YCAL MSS 332: Jonathan Williams & Jargon Society archive.

1968 had finally reached our shores, and a student sit-in at the University of Kent achieves a brief mention in these letters. But perhaps a more consequential invasion over these years was the arrival of French theory, not only in the form of published books but also in the actual shape of the many *maîtres à penser* who crossed the Channel to speak to us. I had secured a Lectureship in History at Kent in 1967, and my earlier experience as a co-editor of *Form* magazine qualified me to take on a leading role in the launching of an interdisciplinary magazine, sponsored by the Faculty of Humanities, entitled *20th Century Studies*. Its expansive and well connected editor, the Italianist Guido Almansi, who contrived to attract both Umberto Eco and Italo Calvino to our editorial board, soon began to absent himself from Kent, and I progressed from being deputy editor to editor.

In 1970, I took on the main responsibility for editing a special number on the subject of Structuralism, and by the end of 1971 I had published a second number on 'Directions in the *nouveau roman*', which included a lengthy interview with Michel Butor. Evidence of these intermittent editorial activities filters through into the Finlay correspondence, not least by way of occasional confessions of falling behind in my replies to his letters. But the clearest sign of a certain contamination between my interest in Structuralist theory and my current interpretation of Finlay's work came in my essay 'Ian Hamilton Finlay: Engineer and Bricoleur', where I borrowed my concepts directly from the anthropologist Claude Lévi-Strauss. This was perhaps the only occasion on which my approach somewhat perturbed Finlay, who mildly suggested that Oscar Wilde was a better reference point for his work than *The Savage Mind*.[11] But the chance of replying to his doubts enabled me to explain to him in my own terms the point that Structuralist theory could be employed to update the basic concepts of classicism. *20th Century Studies* did not of course confine itself to the theories of the moment. In 1974 another special number enabled me to publish for the first time four of Finlay's 'Medallions', which took as their model the relationship of text and image exemplified in the emblem books of early modern Europe.[12]

By no means all my time was taken up by *20th Century Studies*. Among the new universities of the 1960s, Kent had chosen perhaps the most traditional model, with separate colleges that both served as halls of residence and provided teaching space. The Senior Common Rooms brought staff together, whilst the

11. See letter of 30 September 1970 (p. 92).

12. See 'Free-floating metaphor' (introducing *Four Medallions* by Ian Hamilton Finlay), *20th Century Studies* 12, 1964, pp. 64–72. The full series, drawn by Ron Costley and incorporating my commentaries, was later published as *Heroic Emblems* (Z Press, Vermont, 1977).

new teaching programmes encouraged academics of different disciplines to collaborate. Among the personal initiatives that I reported to Finlay were my sponsoring first of a delightful recital of French songs by a Parisian duo ensemble, and secondly of a riveting performance of *Beowulf* in the style of the Japanese Bunraku theatre. A further item, finding an echo in one of Finlay's dreams (more accurately one of his nightmares), was the report of my unofficial programme of the famous silent films of the 1920s, which were borrowed from the BFI and made available for a small fee to staff and students. Perhaps the most serious of all these extra-curricular and curricular activities was my early engagement in the teaching of the Humanities Faculty's MA course on 'The Modern Movement'. Let loose as I was on a yearly round of seminars by my complaisant English colleagues, I began to relish teaching authors who would hardly have found their way into any conventional English literature course at the time: Marcel Proust, Rudyard Kipling and, with special relevance to Finlay, Walter Pater. The fact that Pater's *Imaginary Portraits* was Finlay's 'Favourite Book of All' was impressed upon me. In 1971 this superb collection of essays, which was Proust's favourite also, would be part of my summer reading.[13]

I leave to the reader the task of following the dialogue that is pursued here between such unlikely, but committed, correspondents. Drawing back from the anecdotal detail of our exchanges, I can observe that, in some respects, this whole period was a happy interlude in Finlay's embattled life as an artist. The 'Fulcrum Affair', Finlay's bitter dispute which arose from challenging the improperly so-called First Edition of *The Dancers Inhabit the Party*, had by no means reached a resolution in these years. But it had, for a time, lost the all-consuming intensity that it acquired in the autumn of 1969. Some of the scant news received on this front was good news.[14] Finlay still had intermittent difficulties with his allies and collaborators. There was a brief skirmish with Simon Cutts of the Tarasque group, which was now outgrowing its early roots with a diaspora of its founding members and the admission of talented new artists such as Ian Gardner. Yet Finlay's *Column Poem* was to feature prominently in the

13. See list compiled in November 1970 (p. 99), and letters of 15 July and 20 July 1971 (pp. 140, 142). I had previously been aware only of Pater's essays in *The Renaissance*, of which a copy given to my father in the 1920s had entered my possession. A review of Finlay's library, currently installed at Stonypath by the Little Sparta Trust, shows that he accumulated second-hand Macmillan editions of Pater's major works: *The Renaissance* (1924 edition), *Miscellaneous Studies* (1928), *Marius the Epicurean* (1928), *Appreciations* (1915) and *Imaginary Portraits* (1920).

14. For the ramifications of the dispute, see *Midway* pp. 390–93. The good news, delivered in a letter of 3 April 1971, was that the British Library had confirmed Finlay's view of the status of the Fulcrum edition. Unfortunately the issue arose afresh in the New Year of 1972, and was not finally settled for a further two years.

final Tarasque exhibition of February 1972.[15] The yearly round of the seasons continued to play a major part in respect of the general wellbeing of Finlay and his family. Winter lived up to its reputation of propagating discomfort and disease, and winter had a bad habit of setting in for unforeseen periods in the year. But both in 1970 and in 1971 the arrival of summer initiated a spate of new activities in the garden. Visitors were becoming more and more of a hazard in the late summer months. But, at the very least, they provided confirmation of the fame that had already been achieved by the efforts of the two indigent gardeners.

From my own point of view, the most significant achievement during this period was the completion of my longest essay to date on Finlay's work. He had read, and approved of, my book published in 1970, *Experimental Painting*. But this study of contemporary modes of painting mentioned him only to the extent of illustrating one work that was marginal to my main concerns: his *Wave/Rock* poem on glass from 1966. Finlay received periodic bulletins from me on the slow progress towards publication of my Viking Press anthology, *The Tradition of Constructivism*. Though this was, again, only indirectly related to Finlay's own activities, the New York connection did provide a hot-line to the Librarian of the Museum of New York, Bernard Karpel, who finally (and a little reluctantly) purchased some Wild Hawthorn Press publications. As already noted, my Structuralist essay on Finlay's work received an equivocal response from him. But he was in no doubt at all about the acceptability of the next long piece of writing, which he described on receiving it in late November as my 'essay/monograph' (and occasionally, my 'monologue'). Originally written to accompany an exhibition at the Ceolfrith Gallery, Sunderland, this essay rode the same roller-coaster as the exhibition project, but finally came to rest in a more appropriate location. Douglas Hall, the pioneering Director of the Scottish National Gallery of Modern Art, adopted the whole project and showed Finlay's work in July/August 1972 at the stately Georgian premises of Inverleith House, in the Botanic Gardens of Edinburgh. This exhibition, which covered the full range of his work at the time, moved subsequently to Stirling and to Newcastle.

For Finlay, my essay/monograph 'undoubtedly mark[ed] the New Epoch (of Post-Concrete?)', and managed to 'draw together many threads'. The opening section is reprinted here at the end of our correspondence, since it suggests in what way Finlay's work had come to define the spirit of this 'New Epoch',

15. In my introduction to the exhibition catalogue, I noted Finlay's role in the group's development, while emphasising the independent achievement of Simon Cutts, Stuart Mills and the new adherent, Ian Gardner, who was already becoming one of Finlay's valued collaborators.

against all odds.[16] Finlay compared the general drift of my argument with the message of a letter that he recently received from Jonathan Williams, questioning whether 'The Widest Possible Audience' could 'exist for serious art'.[17] In fact, a particular image had resonated for me throughout the writing of the essay, and this was one that had been generated, and vested with new significance, in the course of our correspondence. On my return from the Loire Valley in the summer of 1971, I had been keen to send Finlay a set of doggerel verses that I had compiled, supposedly in the style of Kipling. These concerned the Viking raids in the early Middle Ages, in response to which a band of monks transported the body of St Philibert from the island of Noirmoutier, off the coast of Brittany, to a safe haven at Tournus in the valley of the Rhône. The refrain of my verses read: 'The ravage of the long ships/ Laid waste Noirmoutier.' Over time, in our later correspondence, those 'long ships' (or 'long boats') began to feature as symbols. In my essay on Finlay, they came to epitomise the contemporary threat to art and culture. The American critic, M. L. Rosenthal, later quoted some of my words, and glossed them, in an article written for the *New York Times Book Review*: '"Finlay's case is precisely that of the traditional culture forced into the small-scale venture and the hazardous channel of communication ... periodically interrupted by the ravages of the long ships". This remarkably accurate formulation *proclaims* as Finlay's achievement what Ezra Pound, in "Mauberley", *feared* would be the outcome of his effort to create a heroic classical art for this century.'[18] Seen from a distance of forty-five years, my judgement still appears to be appropriate when viewed within the context of the times. But it did not take into account the new dimension that would be opened up by Finlay's creation of a garden.

16. See p. 183–86.

17. See p. 169.

18. M. L. Rosenthal, 'The British Poetics', *New York Times Book Review*, 19 January 1975, p. 6.

I

January–December 1970

The previous year had concluded with reminiscences. In his letter to me of 22 December 1969, Finlay welcomed the imminent close of the decade with the message: 'I trust you are remembering that Concrete Poetry (that Movement of the 60's) has but a few days to go ...' Our correspondence had originally begun in September 1964, when, together with my friends at Cambridge, I was involved in organising the first international exhibition of concrete, phonetic and kinetic poetry, held in the Rushmore Rooms of St Catharine's College (28 November–5 December 1964). I also contributed to a special edition of the magazine Image, *on Kinetic art and Concrete poetry, which was published in the same month. There I discussed Finlay's work in a brief article on 'Communication and structure in concrete poetry'. In the mid-60s, Finlay had also developed a strong interest in the devices and structures of kinetic art, while he was gaining his reputation as Britain's leading concrete poet. By the end of the decade, however, he had become increasingly disillusioned with these avant-garde movements, and was seeking to differentiate the direction of his own work from their current tendencies. He had not ceased publishing a stream of poem/prints, cards and booklets. Indeed, the years between 1965 and 1969 were among the most creative periods of his career in that respect. But by 1970 he had begun to embark upon a new artistic strategy. The most striking evidence of this new orientation was to be found in the upland garden which he had begun to develop from 1966 onwards, with the aid of his wife Sue, around the farm of Stonypath, their new home in the Pentland Hills.*

Canterbury
10 January 1970

Dear Ian,

Many thanks for your letter from the last decade, the decade of C * * * P * * *, K * * * A * * *, & one or two other phenomena which are perhaps still with us in a new, Phoenix-like form (viz. John Furnival, who writes to me suggesting a new attempt at the Amber Sands folder which dragged out a lingering demise in 1967–68):[1]

1. The poem had been discussed extensively with Finlay in the mid-1960s. It had been realised as an installation of wooden letter forms (constructed by Kenelm Cox) at the Brighton Festival, April 1967. See *Midway*, pp. 228, pl. 29. John Furnival later proposed using it in a project for his students at Gloucestershire College of Art.

Amber (quick) sands ?
Amber (slow) sands.

And let me welcome with genuine delight the ~ booklet that greeted me on Xmas morning. It is a charming poem, perfectly produced.[2]

How intriguing to hear of the Maltese architect who has bought a wave/rock![3] There must surely be very few of them left by now. So those Scottish museums will be finding their scope rather restricted when they finally come to the point of stocking up with Finlays.

On this particular subject, let me sketch out an idea which occurred to me. I went to call on Jim Ede before Christmas, & found his new Museum extension to Kettle's Yard nearly complete. It will apparently be a fine space for exhibiting, & already is to include a superb Brancusi & a Gabo as well as the collection of Wallis, Nicholson, Christopher Wood. Jim has framed an 'Xmas Star' exceedingly scrupulously and well – & intends to put it just by the entrance to the main gallery.

Now it has always seemed to me that one of your finest works was the column wind/wind – at the same time it is clearly one of the most difficult to situate. How would you like the possibility of me buying the column (taking into account, if that was O.K., the £125 or so that will soon be coming from Kansas for a collection of your letters) & offering it on a semi-permanent loan to the gallery? Of course, I haven't mentioned it to Jim yet, but I could do so without any immediate commitment on either side. It does seem to me so excellent a context for your work – from the point of view of the works around & from that of the numerous young people likely to visit the gallery.[4]

As for the Elizabeth lady, & the publishing world in general – I will certainly pursue the idea of the Poem/prints.[5] But I am coming round to the idea that

2. *Wave*, hand-printed at the Salamander Press, 1969, featured the typographical sign for transposition.

3. The architect John Borg Manduca subsequently collaborated with Finlay on a number of poem/prints, including *Are Aircraft-carriers Urban or Rural* (1976).

4. This plan, welcomed by Finlay, eventually foundered because Jim Ede was doubtful about fitting the work into the collection at Kettle's Yard. See my discussion of our correspondence in *Beauty and Revolution: The Poetry and Art of Ian Hamilton Finlay*, exhibition catalogue, Kettle's Yard, University of Cambridge, 2014, pp. 15–17.

5. For negotiations with Elizabeth Deighton, who worked at the magazine *Studio International*, see *Midway*, p. 404.

something of that kind is more suitable for a folio than a book – & should be undertaken either by such a firm as Alecto or by a private press. What I really mean, I suppose, is that the standard of production required would be so high that it could only be justified if either the prints were indeed prints – & priced accordingly – or the question of expense was itself a secondary one.

All this leads me to ask what exactly were the circumstances of your unfortunate experience with Canterbury College of Art. – I ask because they have a press which I would judge to be most efficient by the evidence of a book of recipes, herbal illustrations & descriptions that has recently reached me. The Principal, whom I meet fairly often, has actually asked me if I could suggest a more inspiring subject for a future volume – & I think that he might well be interested in the Poem/print collection.[6]

So I am really asking who the source of friction was in the previous case – just to be certain that I did not find myself at cross-purposes in proposing it to them.

I've come to the end without mentioning my rapid journey to Paris and back. It was a great success, especially the morning in Chartres which I essayed on the spur of the moment.

Love to Sue, Eck & Ailie. Hope you all recovered entirely from the dire 'flu.

Yours
Stephen

Stonypath
14 January 1970

Dear Stephen,

how very nice it was to get your letter. I look forward – though it seems a peculiar direction to look for it – to Amber Sands. Perhaps our works will always have their first printing when they have come back into Fashion! When I review it I shall say that it reveals your (&) curious cast of mind.

6. Canterbury College of Art was one of several such institutions with which Finlay undertook unsuccessful collaborations in the 1960s, largely because of the latitude which the students took in interpreting his poems. James Martin, the Principal, seemed at this time to offer a better prospect. See also Finlay's response to this query (p. 29).

We are at present engulfed in The Film again.[7] I have long ago lost interest in it; The Director has no control over the cameraman, and the cameraman has the most commonplace Glasgow-Italian type of mind . . . Far from my being allowed to be in charge of the film (as I was originally promised), I have not even seen a foot of it yet, and it is said to be two/thirds completed. The Director whispered to me, today, to ask the cameraman to arrange a showing, as he had asked in vain! With a budget of £3000 one had hoped for more. I feel like asking for some change.

I have – did I tell you – had what I think is a brilliant idea for my Scottish Arts Council poster: Modern British Hangings (sic). I've also had a brilliant idea for adapting Cythera for Galashiels, (did I tell you of that bizarre Competition?): but there is the usual melancholy task of rousing Maxwell [Allan] from his everyday-jobs --- such as the designing of Giant Tombstones for The Central Electricity Board (which may not be quite what he does but is the impression I get . . . .)

Now, as far as I can see, that book of photographs has been abandoned altogether by the photographer. (His name is Ronald Gunn and he ought to be shot.)[8] I had to phone him up to tell him that Dent have selected one of his photos of my Dunfermline show, for the cover of their new Art Annual, edited by Edward Lucie-Smith (which is all I know of it, so far). One might reasonably suppose that this news would have pleased a person who is forever wanting proof of his talents, etc. – but his response was immediate:

"I am getting a little tired of having my photos in these crummy magazines." (Sic)

I was so flabbergasted by this, that I asked Sue to enquire as to whether he still wanted to do the book of photos (which was entirely his idea, as he wrote to the publisher before even consulting me). For what it's worth, he replied that it would be "a great relief not to do it", and that he "had never felt anything about my work". Truly, the course of Post-Concrete Poetry does not run smoothe.

7. For the genesis of this ill-fated project see *Midway*, pp. 364, 373. 'Films of Scotland' had undertaken to make the film, with the aid of funding from the Scottish Arts Council. It was never completed. The first film to record the garden at Stonypath was *Stonypath Days* (1973), shot by James Styles, the photographer attached to the Library of the University of Kent, for which I raised funding of £250 from the Hope Scott Trust.

8. Doubts about the motivation of Gunn had already been expressed in 1969. See *Midway*, pp. 404–5.

Therefore, dear Stephen, will you please ask the Elizabeth lady whether Studio I. would wish to do a book of photos of my poems. Perhaps someone could get off of the single-barrelled Gunn, the photos he **HAS** taken: and these could be supplemented. He certainly had some superb photos. I think this could be a pleasing book.

I might add this little personal plea – that I have **ALMOST** had so many books done in 1969, it would be the greatest pleasure to get one done in 1970.

It would give me great pleasure and encouragement to exchange the Column Poem for that Kansas money. I was awfully cheered by this suggestion* [*very kind]. The poem has survived the Demarco show, and arrived back just before we were snowed-in (we were snowed-in for Ages and Ages, and we still have some of those curious drifts which linger on like David Medallas,[9] here and there, long after the main mud of landscape has returned to view . . .

I must add, though, that I am not sure that Jim Ede would welcome the loan of the Column. I do believe he likes the Xmas Star because it is viewable as an imperfect Wallis (joke) – a sort of boat by an A. Wallis who is unable to draw . . . (further joke). As you know, I am very fond of Jim, and don't in the least mind that he doesn't like my works. But you must not be disappointed, and you will remember that he has that peculiar firmness which is developed by vegetarians through Years of saying No, firmly, to meat-eating Hostesses. Of course, if he was pleased by your suggestion, that would be just grand.

About Canterbury, I can't remember the name of the Typography Teacher (if such he was). I didn't have one of my (I suppose Famous) rows with anyone: it was more that the wretched teacher turned the whole project over to his students, and to a particular student who was – presumably because of his prowess in some other field – such as the football field – placed in charge. I was at some pains to explain my intentions, in each poem, in detail --- and the students, led by this Squint-Letraset-Squadron-Leader, were likewise at some pains – to ignore all I said (and all they had ever learned; it looked like that). The results were hair-raising in their grubby ineptitude, I said so. The Squadron-Leader replied, that if I knew so much about it, I should do it myself . . . .

9. The kinetic artist David Medalla had become well-known in the 1960s for his *Cloud Canyons*, which involved the production of towering columns of white foam.

All the same, being an optimist, I'll back you in any project you like to start there . . . Hope Is My Undoing.

.

However, I would like you to consider very carefully my reasoning on this poem/print project. This is, that if we get the most **PERFECT** folio of prints produced, we will be little further forward, because the immediate need is for establishing the genre – and the way to do this is undoubtedly through a little (or large) book by a proper publisher. I visualise something like one of those little (or large) books devoted to 'Cubism', 'Impressionism', or whatever, with an introduction, and then a certain number of plates, each on the righthand side, facing a page of (specific) explanation and comment, on the left. This, I am sure, is what is tactically needed, now. A publisher, and your splendid and dignified prose – in short, a foundation.

Obviously, a folio is a fine thing, too: but that is something else, again, from this need to fix, establish, explain, **INSERT INTO HISTORY**, a genre that already exists.

Since The Thaw (the non-metaphorical one), we have been busy in the garden, shifting the little-r '**KY**' to a new (and splendid) site; and laying pavingstones (once the floor of the byre) for the new Sundial (which Maxwell [Allan] is reported to be delivering any day now . . .)[10] I have plans, too, for several new poems in stone – with all the Maxwell-problems that always involves . . . And did I tell you I am having my 'Rose Lore' bench carved by another sculptor; so (if he keeps to his promised date) you will be able to sit on 3 Rose Proverbs when you next visit us. Our 130 new trees are all safely planted, too.

All for now. It was jolly nice to hear from you. I hope all goes well with your own projects.

Love,

Aye,
Ian

> pl. 10

10. The 'new' sundial is most probably 'Fragments/Fragrance', to be installed at the front of the house. The 'Rose Lore' bench, undertaken with Vincent Butler, will take its place in the Front Garden before 16 April (see letter, p. 52).

Stonypath
23 January [19]70

Dear Stephen,

it seems ages since I heard from you, though I know it isn't really.

This is an extra letter, really to enclose the green one, and ask what your feelings would be if I suggested to the publisher that they ask you to edit the book on my work – i.e. the possibility 'c' as advanced by them.

There is no mention of money or anything like that, but the first step, anyway, seems to be to write to them with an affirmative answer --- which I have just done; and next, to ask you if you would like to edit the book, something that would please me very much. – We could virtually do the book of photos I have been hoping for, together with other material . . . and all this in a context (or so it seems) of enthusiasm, which was scarcely provided by Mr [Alan] Ross.

Ernst Jandl says the publishers are ex-art students and produce rather lavish books. Their para.3 does suggest we could do something which could inaugurate the Post Concrete Decade!

I would be awfully pleased if you could let me know your feelings more or less by return; I have promised to get in touch again in a few days, with my 'concrete' suggestions re 'a, b, and c'. I need only say how very pleased I would be, to collaborate with you on a project like this.

.

I'm rather depressed at this moment as I've been having an argument with Maxwell [Allan], about the form(s) of stone poems. The basic difficulty is, that he wants everything to be monumental, whereas I want things that will fit into (be assimilated by) a particular environment. The environment I actually have, while the aristocracy fails to buy my work, is Stonypath, which is to say, a cottage garden. This is not a place for monuments.

Another problem is, that I am attracted (nowadays) by very traditional forms – let us say, since it is the particular cause of Maxwell's dissent – a Sundial with a pedastool [sic]. Such a thing, says Maxwell, (in a tight-lipped stonewall way) does not belong to the 20th Century. Which is entirely true: but neither (in a sense) does any Sundial – and Maxwell's own beloved

Roman lettering is scarcely post-Bauhaus. In short, I feel a bit like Picasso, on being told by Rousseau that he (P) was a painter in the old-fashioned manner – or as Derain might have felt if an elderly academician had explained to him that Giotto was old-fashioned and that Mr L David[11] was now the thing . . . In this country, I have never been allowed to know what I am at, till ten years after I have been at it --- and am on something else . . . . Which makes collaboration difficult. It is also a fact that the gift of discussion, or the mutual examination of ideas, is not a strikingly Scottish trait.

A further cause for gloom is, that we were finally allowed to see The Famous Film, the Director wrenching it from the bosom of the cameraman (who was outraged that I should be allowed to see it, uncut, at all). The initial agreement, (when the S. Arts Council provided the £3000) was, that I would have a large say in the making of the film, and that I would see it as we went along . . . In fact, the cameraman was given an entirely free hand, because he made it clear that he would be nasty if he wasn't; while the Director, being more aware of his failures than I was, till recently, did nothing at all . . . and (it must be presumed) hoped for an Angel to descend and put everything right.

The photography is dreadful. It is tolerable where the subject (my wee boats moving on the water, Eck wrecking the pond, real fishingboats) provides the whole content – but where any imagination is needed, it is banal and downright deplorable. All poems are shot (the right word, alas) from directly in front; the camera moves slowly from right to left or advances slowly or retreats slowly --- you have probably been in boats that behaved in this way, hour after hour: it is a tedious thing.

The sheer ineptitude is also astonishing. Where a poem is large, it has to have a child playing in front of it. Where it is small, it has a kitten. – The lawnmower is filmed exhaustively. Sue is pictured at length, removing driftwood from the pond. The grand opening shot (to accompany the subtitle) is of KY 365,[12] balanced at an acute angle on a rock on the edge of the sea, straight on (of course) so that it appears to be a cardboard shipwreck. Behind this is a battleship (a well-known Finlay theme).

Nothing has been thought about, or felt, or understood. And it seems that the whole £3000 has already been spent, or virtually so --- the Director is too

11. I.e. the French neo-classical painter, Jacques-Louis David.

12. A painted wooden structure based on a fishing-boat registration sign, dating from 1969.

frightened of the cameraman (who has the contract) to enquire (he says quite openly, as if this were the most natural thing . . .)

There is the raw start of about 9 different films. One could make 3 of them, given 5 filming days to get the material – and a cameraman who did as he was told.

As it is, I have given my opinion, and my attitude is now going to be, **NO TAXATION WITHOUT REPRESENTATION**. – The waste is horrifying. I don't think anything can be done.

The fact is, that these people are just not grown up enough to make a work of art. They lack talent, but that is not the key thing, because one could make quite a nice film with a talentless cameraman if it was understood that his limitations had to be respected, instead of having to be pandered to, as now. No, it is a question that these people have their attention on money, and status, and personalities (theirs), and not at all on the work of art (which is merely a means). Now a reasonable film is not all that hard to make, but it's not going to happen by chance. They behave as if one could make a film with less energy than it takes to work a shift as a bus-conductor (which is quite a hard thing to do – but Life is hard for many people).

I must say I would have liked to try (at least) to make a half-decent little film – but this disaster was obviously coming, and here it now is . . . And still the Director wont take any responsibility, as if Magic is going to put everything right before he finally has to show the film to the S. Arts C.

So what can one do? If the cameraman can't be told when a shot is not good enough, (because his personality wouldn't allow criticism), there just can't be a film.

It is too depressing to think about . . .

·

I hope you are fine, Stephen. And look forward to hearing from you.

Love,
Ian

Canterbury
26 Jan[uary] [19]70

Dear Ian,

This is really a reply by return, as I have just returned an hour or two ago from a quiet weekend in Arundel in Oliver [Hawkins]'s new house. I am absolutely delighted to find so pleasant enthusiastic and business-like a letter from Kohlkunstverlag, especially as the kind of book that they envisage seems to be the kind of book that we would both prefer. (My only momentary qualm was produced by a too hasty first reading of the green letter, which seemed to imply that the book was to be made out of that self-same paper – which, when boiled for several hours, makes passable spinach). If I may suggest it, the book could be a Finlay-reader which kept away from the traditional chronological ordering, and concentrated upon the course of your work as – to borrow my own term – the creation of a universe.[13] The effect of the book would reside in its entirety, and I could make intermittent textual stitches, as well as a fairly long discursive piece to provide a basis of unity.

However I must not expatiate to the extent of missing the post. The letter, which I enclose, seems too good to be real, but I have no doubt that it is so, especially when vouched for by Ernst Jandl.

I must simply add that the 'lanes' poem is giving me great pleasure,[14] and I will write very soon the letter that I had been going to write. Your film story is saddening. I shall have to make the saga of Scottish non-communication even more bitter by sending you a quote from D. Hume (found in Gibbon's *Autobiography*) in which he remarks with some surprise the appearance of *Decline and Fall* in so barbarous a country as England, where, in contra-distinction to Scotland, men of letters had for some twenty years abjured polite communication . . .

Love to Sue, Eck, and Ailie

Yours
Stephen

13. Cf. the title of my article on Finlay's work in *Studio International* (January 1969).

14. *Lanes*, with drawings by Margot Sandeman, hand-printed by the Salamander Press, 1969.

Stonypath
12 February 1970

Dear Stephen,

I am always hoping to have the letter you spoke of . . . This, I hasten to say, is not to be interpreted as a criticism, but as an appreciation. There is no-one whose letters I look forward to more.

I was delighted to have your assurance of interest in the German book. I wrote at once, giving them your name and address, and saying I hoped they would be in touch with you. I haven't heard since, but I suppose it is not very long, really.

I had a letter from Robert Creeley, containing a carbon of a letter he had just sent to Montgomery, protesting at his treatment of 2 American poets. And containing the astonishing news that A. Ginsberg had begun to circulate a petition on behalf of one of the poets, and against Montgomery . . . It is fascinating to speculate on the conflicts which that news will arouse in the London Underground (so to speak).

Stephen, what do you think of the idea of your writing a wee letter to: Mr J H Martin, Editor, Ships Monthly, Endlebury Publishing Company Limited, Grosvenor Road, E.10 --- and asking if you might do a short, profusely illustrated piece on my more nautical postcards and prints . . . This magazine is rather nicely produced, and the editorials are often surprisingly erudite, making passing references to 'The Wasteland', or Aldous Huxley . . . I thought the article might make a pleasing variation on those on figureheads (for instance) – and would introduce our prints to a new public. My special reason for suggesting it is, that I have embarked on several new prints, including a sequel to Xmas Star,[15] and it often seems to me that there must be a literate, non-literary public which might enjoy these. The article would perhaps not be a great chore for you, as it could be brief and straightforward.

I had a pleasing letter from Swallow Press, about my contribution to their Modern British Poetry anthology. They are reproducing 5 or 6 poem/prints in full colour, as well as a photo of '**KY**' in full colour[16] . . . and several full-page black and w. photos . . . They apologised for having to leave two items out . . . .

15. This was to be Poem/print No. 14, *Xmas Rose*, with John Furnival (1970).

16. The 'KY' concrete construction had been photographed in colour in the course of Finlay's exhibition at Pittencrieff Park, Dunfermline (April 1969). See *Midway*, pl. 25.

We have got to know a new photographer, a lassie, who I hope will be a much more pleasant companion than that wretched (double-barrelled) Gunn.[17] (May Disaster fall on his lenses).

Hope all is well with you. Do write! Love,

Ian

Canterbury
16 February 1970

Dear Ian,

Here is another letter on the *20th Century Studies* paper. It is very overdue, & that is partly a result of the claims of the said *20th Century Studies*, which is preparing an edition on the mysteries of Structuralism. I have spent what seemed like days & were certainly mornings and afternoons almost literally wrestling with foreign obscurities. It always quite surprises me when what I translate actually turns out to be fairly readable English – since there is such a thing as a French thought (even, sad to relate, a Belgian thought) which resists transplantation to our soil.[18]

It is good to hear that you have replied to the Kohlkunstverlag, & I hope they will swiftly reciprocate. I have had a rather involved and occasionally three-cornered negotiation with Viking over the past few weeks. It hinges upon a certain non-reciprocity between us – in the sense that I never quite fully reply to their letters, & they never quite reply to mine. But in spite of this, the Constructivism anthology is proceeding handsomely. In fact they may even be able to bring it out by the end of the summer. I was rather pleased to get a letter from Bernard Karpel ('possibly the foremost bibliographer of modern art') who is effusively enthusiastic about the collection – & sees it occupying the 'same central place' in this batch of 'Documents of Modern

17. The photographer mentioned here for the first time is Diane Tammes, who took many notable photographs of Stonypath in the years that followed.

18. My preoccupation with the issue of *20th Century Studies* on 'Structuralism' (May 1970) certainly accounted for any delay in writing this letter. In addition to an essay of my own, this issue contained 'The problem of literary structuralism', by the Belgian scholar François Van Laere, which I had the ungrateful task of translating.

Art' as the Motherwell 'Dada painters and poets' did in the 1950's batch.[19] Luckily, they are anxious to include quite a number of photographs & line drawings –

I wonder if I thanked you for *Lanes* – I do so very gratefully once again or for the first time as the case may be. Isn't it maybe an English poem? Even a Surrey poem? (Home counties at any rate). That would be one's conclusion up to the point of the White Rose – at that stage, I don't know.

It's an excellent idea to approach the Editor of *Ships Monthly*. I would be very willing to do the kind of article you suggest. And of course I look forward with pleasant anticipation to the new prints.

I have a feeling that *Field* may eventually appear before the next few weeks are out. It has dragged rather for the last month or so. But then Stuart [Mills] had had quite enough to think about à propos of Luke. He says that Luke is like a Kenneth Martin, which is a very good description for a baby, considering the twisting backwards and forwards that they do.[20] I shall in all probability be going to see the real Kenneth Martins some time before the end of term, having just corresponded with him about a photo for the Viking book.

Did I tell you that I shall be in Venice again for the Easter vacation? That is, all but a concluding week back here in preparation for next term. I have not yet determined how to vary my repertory in accordance with the demands of the new audience, but, as far as I record, the advertised programme culminates in 'Vasarely: Ian Hamilton Finlay'. I got some slides made from those beautiful colour photos of the first big group of poem constructions.[21] Their crisp Nordic luminosity is a refreshing tonic in the slightly overripe Venetian atmosphere.

I must now prepare in a quiet way for, of all things, a seminar on Karl Marx.

19. Karpel, who was Librarian of the Museum of Modern Art, New York, had been given the task of compiling an extensive bibliography for my collection, *The Tradition of Constructivism*. The expectation that the book would be published in 1970 was wide of the mark, since it was delayed until 1974.

20. The painter and sculptor Kenneth Martin, who contributed a text to my anthology, was creating a series of small mobiles involving spiralling movement throughout this period.

21. Photographs taken by R. L. Williamson in 1968 (see *Midway*, pls 21, 22).

Hoping that the weather is not proportionately more bitter & unfriendly than it is down here, & with love to Sue, Eck & Ailie,

Yours
Stephen

Snow Wednesday [pm 19 February 1970]
Stonypath

Dear Stephen,

here we are, snowed-in again. Your letter was brought up by the shepherd, who had trudged through the drifts between here and Anston. It is splendid to hear from you.

A Belgian thought – is indeed a thought. I can imagine its colour – a kind of purple, shading off into yellow . . . Have you noticed those astonishing Belgian colour-schemes which recur in their art? They are what Spengler might have termed: The hues of the boiled sweetie of the Northern Plain. (Do you have boiled sweeties in England?)

Since I last heard from you, and greatly to our delight and surprise, (not to mention relief), we had a cheque from Kansas – really yours, for the letters.[22] It was something of a coincidence since I had just written them – for the first time in years – to ask if they would like to buy some of my (I mean other people's) early concrete booklets – those which I don't wish particularly to re-read. I can scarcely hope to tell you how very welcome this money was, as we are getting staggering bills by every post – the consequence, of course, of my having started work again: did I not work we could scrape along without those awful crises. It is really and truly generous of you, to have had this money directed to us, and we appreciate it very much and do not in the least take it for granted.

I had already removed the Column Poem from the gallery, and when you next write, you can let me know whether you would like us to send it to you, or whether you feel you might be able to take it, on your next visit. I feel that

22. The payment was for a second batch of the letters written to me by Finlay in the mid-1960s. These were published in *Midway*, by courtesy of Special Collections, Library of the University of Kansas (see also *Midway*, p. 15).

the latter would be safer, if we thoroughly wrapped it in blankets or something. It is a little long, but could, I am sure, be manuouvred [sic] onto the Dunsyre bus – and then put in the train's van, with a wee lecture to the Guard. However, if you would prefer us to crate it, and send it by road, we will . . . .

I'm glad your Constructivism book is getting on so well (touch wood). I cannot resist using that sentence as an opening to this paragraph, because it now goes on to inform you . . . that you are to appear in The Puffin Book of Verse and Fun, and will be hearing from the Editor, Geoffrey Summerfield, shortly; I have just supplied him with your address. Congratulations – and may you have many further successes in this field.[23]

Geoffrey Summerfield is a new contact (odious word), who seems most friendly, and open to all manner of suggestions. Had I mentioned him before?

From Constructivism, to Bernard Karpel. Stephen, could you – and I say this with the utmost urgency – make a very special point (even if it should be a little awkward) of writing to Mr Karpel about my poem/prints . . and our other Wild Hawthorn productions. We had a tenuous contact with him at one time, but he left for an extended stay in Japan . . and that was that. The Museum of M. A., does not have any of our recent prints*[*or postcards] (if indeed it has any at all) – or of my publications over the past years, and it is such an impersonal organisation that I have never seen a way of getting in proper touch with it. There is no doubt that they ought to have my stuff – and indeed, I see no reason why you shouldn't ask them to do an exhibition of poem/prints in general, and a volume on the subject! I think it is not entirely wishful thinking to say, that they would be interested if they knew enough to know they ought to be . . . and Constructivism may have provided you with a chance to tell them.

This is not a random request, as I have been intending to ask your aid in a renewed onslaught on the public citadels. We are again having a money-crisis, or rather, a whole series of them, and this is simply because I am not able to sell my work. I know how much better it is, than a great deal that is sold, and

23. Geoffrey Summerfield, who was at the time a Senior Lecturer at the University of York, published a number of anthologies of poems intended for children during this period. These included *Creatures Moving* (Penguin Education, 1970), which featured work by Edwin Morgan and Jonathan Williams. However, I can find no trace of this Puffin book project, and assume that it was never published.

I get very exasperrated [sic] at my own inability to make a wee tour of Europe, go to see galleries, and museums, and solve the problem once and for all. The stark, or brute, fact is that my poems and prints, now cost between £50 and £120 each to produce. I only have to start working regularly, to bankrupt us all – and the poem/prints, at least, ought to sell without undue difficulty, now. There is also the point that I am not going to live forever and must get on with whatever I have to do.

So I am again racking my brains to think how the problem may be eased. With the children, Sue has little time to work at the Wild H., and anyway, we somehow are not adapted to the world of booksellers and pushing limited editions and so on. The answer must lie in attracting the attention – but no, there's the rub, because that's exactly what I have an impulse to avoid nowadays . . . I can't do lists which sell books: lists that list them are all I can manage. But a single person, a Karpel, or a suitable dealer, could solve the entire problem overnight by 'taking up' my work. Ten years from now is going to be too late: I need to sell now, so I can afford to keep on working.

On an allied theme, Stuart [Mills] told me of the depressing TLS Round-Up on Recent Concrete.[24] In fact, I have not sent any of our productions to the TLS for a very long time, for Mr Willett's slick idiocies became more than I could well stomach . . . but when I reflect on the toil – and that is the word – I have had, in the last few years, to expand concrete poetry in various directions, in a decent way, I could almost weep to hear that 'standards' are lacking and are to be provided by Messrs. Rot and Mayer. [Dieter] Rot is just that, and Hansjorg is a nice, hard-working chap who has little to say except a certain youthful energy . . . The idea that either Hansjorg or Rot have produced anything near (in quality) some of my recent poem/prints, or the final version of 'seiner/silver', or certain of the stone poems, or the glass 'wave/rock', is simply absurd. I do not say this in jealousy; I know what is right and what is wrong. It is true that I already knew J.W. is stupid, and that I expected no better --- but it is also true that one must rely on TLS comment for sales and status --- which is to say, for the wherewithal to keep working. Rely on the TLS or find an alternative – which I am trying to do . . . but I am not good at such things.

24. John Willett had opted to review a selection of publications from the past few years in a full-page article entitled 'Recent combings from the Concrete Fringe' (*TLS* 3546, 12 February 1970, p. 182).

I do wish, though, that someone would finally put J.W. in his place: such crass stupidity coupled with such arrogance is scarcely to be tolerated, even if one doesn't have to read the rubbish oneself . . .

Standards, indeed.

·

You had certainly thanked me for 'Lanes'. It is not an English poem but a Fife one: as you never visited us in Coaltown you do not know how remarkably pastoral that part of the world – with its red-tiled cottages in tumbledown lanes – can be.[25]

Jolly good if you write to Ship's Monthly. I'm probably the only ex-concrete poet who would think of it, and you are the only critic who would wish to do it . . . I often think that it's because we have such universal orientations that we have such small success in particular fashions: we are so open that we earn the reputation of being pig-headed fanatics.

·

I had a reply from the German publisher today, saying that they are now preparing a contract, and approve my idea of doing the book as a bi-lingual edition (they had suggested English only, where I feel that would be needlessly limiting their audience. They also – thank heavens – approve my nomination of you as Editor; and their only, and rather irritating, demur, is at the idea of your writing a long introduction. I am going to write back immediately, and explain politely – what I think is the case – that we have a perfect understanding and that you have a great gift of writing precise prose of the sort I can't, and that this is the perfect and proper foil to my own reductive method. They will, I hope, see this when I put it all more explicitly and forcibly: I by no means want your editing restricted from the outset: I think that our scheme is not only practical but matches theirs better than they realise. At any rate, they have accepted you as Editor, and now I must get the outlines properly laid down, and have them write to you direct.

Let me know when you are going to Venice in advance – all those gondolas without any airships.

25. See *Midway*, pp. 135–57, for the Finlays' brief stay at Coaltown of Callange, Ceres, Fife, in the summer of 1966.

(By the way, I am building a vast glider, which should be ready before your visit: it will stun – so to speak – any sheep, on whose woolly bottom it lands.)

We have been snowed-in so much, that it is scarcely sure how this letter will reach a Post Office . . .

Keep well; write soon. Aye,

Ian

PS I forgot to say that I have got in touch with an English woodcarver (craftsman) who is making me a new boats-as-seasons – the third in the series – sundial.[26] My plan is to have it carved in a huge piece of timber – it is actually going to be oak – which will be thrust vertically into the ground. I have not of course seen any of this chap's carving yet, but the letters I have had from him are most encouraging. They are – it is worth remarking – the very opposite thing from that represented by Montgomery (etc.): masculine letters, simple and direct, and yet with a clear sensitivity to the end in view. They are so refreshing – and it is only when one comes up against this type of sensibility, that one realises (again) how rare it is and how valuable it is, too. I'm afraid it is not a literary type of sensibility, but there is no reason why it should be tied to a craft: it is a type of sensibility which could as well make books, poems, or even laws . . . . Jolly nice to come across, simply, through answering an Advertisement in 'The Dalseman' (sic).[27]

Canterbury
7 March [1970]

Dear Ian,

Many thanks for your letter. Now it is me who is snowed in, or nearly so. Kent had had its proverbial dose of early-Spring snow, & villages and miners have been left in jeopardy. What is more, we have had (still have) a

> pl. 7, 8, 9

26. The wood-carver in question was John R. Thorpe. His sundial 'The Four Seasons as Fore-And-Afters' was installed at Stonypath by September 1971, but it was later removed. Thorpe worked in the Yorkshire Dales, and was also responsible for the memorable 'Evening will come' sundial.

27. Finlay's *sic*, but the publication is *The Dalesman*.

sit-in of what my mother calls 'ignorant and mutinous' students in a central building of the university. So the theme of beleaguerment is a dominant one these days . . .

However I have been able to make quite frequent excursions to the outside world. Last week I was in Aberystwyth for 36 hours (that is, including the travel there and back). It was incredibly long & progressively more risqué journey – in the sense that by the time that one got to Shrewsbury, one was almost at the limits of possibility – & the passage through Montgomeryshire (across Offa's dyke) seemed entirely unreal. There is something about Wales – which is not at all paralleled in Scotland – that gives the impression of extreme unreality. This was not at all diminished by the strangeness of Aberystwyth, where I had cream buns in the Caprice Café, Chinese food on the promenade, and delivered a lecture on constructive art to a slightly bemused audience at a great rate (speed, not fee, that is). On Monday I shall be giving it in a rather more leisurely form, I think, to a Cambridge audience.[28]

It was good to hear of the arrival of the cheque from Kansas.[29] I'm particularly glad that it will help with the resumed work. When I was last in touch with the Kansas people, they said they would like to have carbons of my letters to you if they existed. Of course they don't (& I somehow have a great antipathy to taking carbons of things – only equalled by my antipathy to those sinister Xerox-copied things). But I said to them that it might be possible to take some kind of copy some time.

Jim Ede wrote back immediately about the column poem & was very appreciative of my suggestion. – & felt that he had two positions that might accommodate the poem. But he did say, as we expected, that he would have to see it before making a definite acceptance. I don't feel it will photograph well – so the solution would probably be, as you suggest, to wait for a car from Stonypath to the South. I shall in all probability call on Jim in Cambridge on Monday. He said, by the way, that he was very satisfied with the Xmas Star, though whether it is in lieu of a Wallis I wouldn't like to say!

28. I had been invited to speak to the Cambridge University Visual Arts Society by David Mayor, who was then a student but would later be associated with the Beau Geste Press at Exeter, and became an expert on the Fluxus Group.

29. This was the second occasion on which I had sold a batch of letters written to me by Finlay during the 1960s to the University of Kansas. The correspondence was published in *Midway* (see also p. 38).

Geoffrey Summerfield sent me a request to reprint the poem in question & I had a moment of exquisite doubt in pondering the precise amount of guineas to settle upon![30]

I shall be writing to Karpel shortly, and will be sure to mention your recent work to him – certainly the Museum should be collecting it. As for what you say about a possible dealer, would you consider the possibility of me approaching the London Graphic Arts Gallery, a representative of which I met fairly recently? They are evidently a highly progressive organisation, with permanent exhibitions touring this country and the U.S.A. Also they are particularly concerned with graphics, & so do not regard them as a mere complement to more expensive works.

I must pack up and leave for London now, in preparation for Cambridge. I shall be seeing Kenneth Martin for lunch at his studio & then taking tea at the Ritz with R[obert] Motherwell[31] –

Love to Sue, Eck & Ailie,

Yours
Stephen

PS I go to Venice two weeks from now – March 22.
Hope to hear that the German contract is proceeding.

Stonypath
15 March 1970

Dear Stephen,

it was a great shock to me, to learn from your letter that there are coal-mines in Kent. It is exactly as if I had noticed a pit-bing in the

30. The poem was my 'Landscape of St Ives, Huntingdonshire', first published in *Poor. Old. Tired. Horse.*, No. 25 (1967), and later issued as the first in the series of my poem cards published by Tarasque Press in 1970.

31. Both these meetings were in the line of my continuing work as editor of *The Tradition of Constructivism.* Martin contributed his text, 'Construction from within'. The American Abstract Expressionist painter Robert Motherwell had launched the original series of 'Documents of 20-Century Art' with his collection, *The Dada Painters and Poets*, and was General Editor of the new volumes published by Viking Press, New York. He subsequently apologised for having been a victim of food poisoning at the time of this meeting.

background of a [Samuel] Palmer landscape. --- I trust you are un-snowed by now. I have to confess that I take a Scotch view of English snow, as something essentially flippant, relating to fancy rather than the imagination. Do not, however, think I am decrying the drifts you had. They certainly caused a flurry.

Your mother's phrase, ignorant and mutinous, (of the students) is superb. Has she read Yeats, do you suppose?[32] As I write, it is mid-morning, but the sky is overcast, and an ignorant and mutinous twilight still prevails.

Alphabet Poem

Aberystwyth

Re your letters and Kansas, that university, or at least Mr Williams, is quite disconcerting, as it obviously has a wee interest in me, but it never answers my letters, just not at all, since several years. This makes communication chancy.

The Column Poem has been sent South with Stuart, yesterday, as I judged that any progress in that direction, was to the good – (the high road to England, etc.). It went with DRIFT, which has been bought by the Contemporary Arts Society, via Nigel Greenwood, Free Lance Art Agent.[33] The Column Poem is carefully wrapped in a green bedspread, and I thought of adding an Instruction saying:

For Pop Art shows, exhibit as is

For Concrete shows, please unwrap

– but you know what concrete shows are nowadays: so I didn't bother. I am rather nervous of Jim Ede's verdict, but we'll see what he says.

We had a nice weekend with Stuart [Mills] --- wrecking in one-and-a-half days, three month's (spelling, or is it grammar) of gliders and sailplanes. The large ones, which I launch from 3 yards of elastic, tied to 30 feet of thread, are truly spectacular: I will give you a demonstration when you come to see us.

32. My mother (and father) had indeed read Yeats. They named their first house after his well-known poem on the 'lake-isle' of Innisfree.

33. Nigel Greenwood had worked previously at the Axiom Gallery, London. For the tensions between him and Finlay at the time of the one-man show of Finlay's work at the gallery in 1968, see *Midway*, pp. 339–40.

It would be interesting to know the fees stipulated to Geoffrey Summerfield, by all the One-Word-Bards. My friend Astrid (Gillis) was considering asking for a bunch of flowers, for her two little ones . . . My 'Air Letters' (which is to go in complete) certainly deserves a quite expensive Glider Kit. Whatever you asked for St. Ives, I'm sure you will actually GET a view of that town, done in marquetry.

R. Motherwell. Well, well. The Ritz. Words fail me.

In the Ritz
No-one spits.
The drinking and eating
Is done in surroundings of exquisite luxury, with
                    lashings of grub and so on, and
                                        commodious seating.

And superb conversation, too, I am sure. – It is one of life's little ironies that Motherwell is, so to speak, the Scottish Pittsburgh. (Spelling?)

I hope you got the two pc's I sent fairly recently, the shell-hued one, and the red one . . . .

Our troubles with the Axiom are not yet over. Having sold the wave/rock to Mario Amaya's[34] Ontario Gallery, and having been paid for it months ago, they simply wont send me the cheque. Neither will they send the money they owe us for prints sold. They do not apologise or make excuses: they simply don't pay, as if Robbery is their Right. The London Scene really seems extraordinary.

All the same, Stephen, if you could speak (as you suggest) to the London Graphic Arts Gallery, I would be most grateful. And Mr Karpel too. I know these things are chores but they would be immensely appreciated.

Karpel, in your garden pond or lake . . .

(As Apollinaire sang, in translation . .)[35]

34. The critic and curator Mario Amaya had been Editor of the periodical *Art and Artists* in Britain in the 1960s.

35. The reference is to the French poet Guillaume Apollinaire's *Bestiary* (*Le Bestiaire*), and his verse on 'The Carp', which begins (in a variant translation): 'In your pools, and in your ponds,/ Carp, you indeed live long'.

I WHOLLY share your antipathy to those "sinister Xerox-copied things". The only good Xerox is the Zuyder Zea Rocks.[36]

Now Stephen, could I ask you a wee favour – or at least one that wont, I hope, prove too large . . . It is this: You will remember my Land/Sea 'semiotic' poem/print, and it is my intention to use this as the basis of a Sundial.[37] My idea is, to use one of the splendid dials I have obtained via my architect friend in Pilkington Glass – a dial which looks itself like a net

– that sort of effect, the horizontal lines indicating the positions of the gnomon's shadow, in terms of length, on certain dates . . so the dial would show the time and the date of the month (on certain dates) . . . while by adding the key

SEA —
LAND /

the lines will serve the same semiotic purpose as those in the original print. Now it [is] my intention (or Hope) to do the Sundial as a screenprint on cardboard, which the reader (?) will cut out and fold, for his domestic use. This will involve an instruction sheet, and on this sheet I would like to put (add) a small paragraph, signed by you, of the sort you added to The Blue and Brown calendar . . . really 'explaining' the poem. What I would like you to explain, very briefly, is the nature of the semiotic poem in general; also briefly, the idea of land and sea as a network, with perhaps a reference to the 'net' in my work in general (i.e. the Signpost net/planet poem, the NETS weathercock) . . and then, finally, some brief reference to the – still slightly staggering to me! – notion of a Land/sea Sundial which tells the time and registers the shadow's length at specific dates. Incidentally, solar time is what's used on the dial.

36. Possibly a reference to the fact that in the Zuyder Zea (the large area of sea water reclaimed by the Dutch) there are no rocks.

37. The original poem/print bearing this title was designed in collaboration with Herbert Rosenthal, and published in 1967. The renewed use of this concept, which benefitted from the skills of Michael Harvey, led eventually to the creation of the Canterbury Sundial in 1972. > pl. 3

Such a paragraph, in your elegant prose, will enhance greatly the whole assemblage – and I will, if I may, pay you in sundials. (You will surely become the first person **EVER** to be paid in sundials?) While I know that you are always very busy, it would be very cheering if you could manage the para. before too long, as it encourages me to believe in projects when I have all the elements (and they are often **MANY!**) to hand, at the start . . .

It is, I think, a very nice idea, and I would aim to do the whole thing in the most elegant way . . . in a limited edition of (perhaps) 100 copies . . .

Do you think you could manage such a paragraph?

·

I have just had (not for the first time) a very un-nerving experience with John Furnival, who can do very nice things sometimes, but is deplorably careless at others – on (I always feel) Moral Principle (since to care is nowadays considered wicked). Anyway, not only did he not meet the deadline promised (by him to me, and by me, in turn, to the Scottish Arts Council), he produced lettering which disjointed space and made me cross-eyed just looking at it – simply because he found that the lettering he'd done, didn't fit the space and couldn't be bothered re-doing it . . . This kind of thing is beyond me. It is one of the few commissions I have ever had, and my entire payment (though not John's) will have to go on having a commercial artist re-do (on transparencies) the layout I have made from John's . . It is most irritating. He also did that **INFURIATING** thing of hand-drawing half the letters and then – getting bored, or finding that lunch was ready – doing the rest in Squint Letraset (a thing that drives me **FRANTIC**). Further, he did not (of course) bother to **RETURN** the text he was given . . which is a habit of artists of the **NEW** School . . . and he has (I notice) got the exhibition in question opening at 2 a.m. which seems very unlikely indeed, in the case of a Scottish Arts Council show. Grrrr . . . . However, I still have hopes of getting the thing properly realised. How sad that one so often ends up by getting a commercial artist to tidy up after the Altruists – and put a bit of honest care into the job. Do you know what I mean? I am quite serious: ones like John actually think it is morally wicked to **CARE** about deadlines (i.e. **PROMISES**) and things being right . . . Hence Stuart Montgomery, the inevitable by-product of Ealing Bhuddism [sic].

End of tirade, but not of pain arising from its cause.

Your example is better appreciated (more **DEEPLY**, that is) than you realise.

Love,

Ian

All in all, I would easily forgive the errors, but I resent the idea that I am wicked or eccentric to want a thing to be as right as it can be.

P.S. Stephen, did you write to *Ships Monthly*?

Canterbury
[mid-March 1970]

Dear Ian,

In extreme rapidity (I am about to hover across the Channel) here is a little piece for the projected assemblage.

'The net, or network, is today an indispensable concept for the semiologist, or student of the science of signs. Its proper purpose would be to denote a limited or provisional capture of meaning, through the application of a pre-established grid.

For Ian Hamilton Finlay, the net serves both as an indication of a poetic procedure analogous to that of semiology, & also as a concrete image, annexed to the world of the ocean and the fishing boat. In his recent Land Weathercock, the four cardinal points – **NESW** – were replaced by the letters **NETS**.[38] Thus the variable field covered by the pointer was equated with the sum of the various fishing fields at different points of the compass.

In this particular work, Finlay returns to a theme which he used earlier for a poem-print: that of a network of lines to indicate (when interpreted by a semiotic key) the interrelations of sea and land. But this network is also a sundial, upon which horizontal lines indicate the position of the gnomon at various times of the year. Thus the opposition sea/land is supplemented by that between sea/land & sky. Finlay establishes this triangular linkage, which can also be found in earlier work, with particular elegance and formal economy.'

38. Illustrated in *Midway*, pl. 11.

From tomorrow, I am at:
PENSIONE ALLA SALUTE
DORSODURO
VENICE

Yours
Stephen

Pensione alla Salute
Venice
7 April 1970

Dear Ian,

Venice, as usual, has taken away my impulse to communicate with the external world, & I find myself leaving till my last day here the letter I promised you on the point of boarding my Hoverkraft.

Incidentally, the experience of travelling across the Channel in the said Hoverkraft was an undignified but absorbing one. The Hoverkraft creates a cloud of spray, under cover of which it advances like a dyspeptic crab. Then, having alighted on the apron, it subsides gradually with a noise of progressive deflation until it rests with seeming innocence, ready for the next departure.

Venice is full of more comely craft – it is particularly pleasant because of the presence of a fleet of sturdy & brightly painted tugs (with names like STRENUUS) which haul in the battered cargo vessels & tankers. In keeping with the maritime mood, I included in one of my lectures a complete set of slides of Ocean Stripe 5, which went down very well. It was particularly useful as my valiant attempt to speak the Schwitters postscript[39] in a previous (Dada) lecture had caused a little flurry of aesthetic doubt.

I have also had a weekend in Vienna, where the celebrated café of the Wiener Gruppe was pointed out to me. It was very gloomy to look at compared with my favourite Venetian café, Florian's in St Mark's Square, where Proust sat correcting his translation of Ruskin & where I sit consuming an occasional Zabaglione confected from Marsala & yolks of egg. As I plan to return to

39. Kurt Schwitters's phonic poem *W W PBD*, which was republished in *Form* 3 in 1966, had been printed also as a 'Postscript' to Finlay's *Ocean Stripe 5* (1967).

England via Paris, & the West of France, my Spring itinerary will have come to look like the flight of an ecclesiastical butterfly – with the weekends providing successively Bach at Canterbury, the Easter Vigil in St Mark's, Palestrina in St Stephen's Cathedral, Vienna, & finally (I hope) the Choir of St John's, Cambridge, in Chartres –

I hear news from home about the appalling English weather. No doubt Scotland has surpassed all that Suffolk and Yorkshire could provide. I travelled through the Alps to get to Vienna & found drifts of snow at fairly low altitudes – & finally it snowed about four times whilst I was in the city itself. Luckily Venice is far enough away from any mountains not to be affected.

I wondered while I was in Vienna whether it might have been remotely possible to speak to the Kohlkunstverlag man. But I should think that things are not yet at the stage where that would have been useful. Anyhow, if I remember rightly, the main department is in Frankfurt?

I hope you found the hurried note acceptable for the new Sundial/Land/sea. If not, I can reword it or revise it entirely.

I must now leave in preparation for the festivities of our last evening in Venice.

Love to Sue, Eck & Ailie,

Yours

Stephen

Stonypath
16 April 1970

Dear Stephen,

I have been delighted to hear from you and have only put off writing because I haven't been sure when you'd be back in Canterbury, and I remember sad experiences of letters being returned from there, HOUSE EMPTY. Perhaps you are safely home now --- though I get the impression that you are starting to regard Venice as your true home, or at least home-from-home. ("Zabaglione!" exclaimed Sir Jaspar, "tis a comely yolk of egg . .")

Anyway, your letters are delightful, as always, thank you. And the little prose piece for the cardboard sundial, is just the thing – if you will allow me to remove a sentence of too-explicit praise of my work. These sundials are going to take a wee while to realise, as there is so much preparatory work to be done, but they are a jolly good idea, and having all the written material to hand, is the first essential, if one is to think seriously about the later stages, and the mundane problems connected with cardboard.

My model for the Galashiels competition has gone off, and I must say it looks jolly good. It is Cythera, done as a mosaic pool, with a pergola rising from its sides (and punctuating the poem with its square pillars). The whole (except of course the pergola) is realised in mosaic – even in the model; and the effect is very posh, and most Watteau-esque: I do declare no-one would blink if I claimed it had been in an attic since the 18th century . . . Maxwell [Allan] excelled himself, however, in the non-collaborationing of which he is capable, and once threw down the phone when I dared (7 weeks after the promised deadline) to enquire, very politely, when the model might be ready . . . I scarcely suppose the poem will prove acceptable to Galashiels, but the model will remain with the S. Arts Council, and something may come of it.

I have also been having awful troubles with John Furnival, but I think I mentioned those, and the exhibition which he contrived to have opening – in sedate Edinburgh – at 2 a.m. . . John is one of those (alas numerous) people who believe in detachment – especially in detachment from the needs of others, and of course from standards. Posterity will be puzzled that he did such fine things with me, and such really frightful things for himself.

> pl. 4

My little marble tombstone-poem is now up, in the garden,[40] as is the Rose Lore Stone Bench. You will see them when you come.

As regards the German publisher, he finally sent a sample publication, (which he has oddly asked me to return, as he has no more of them, he says), and when I had looked at it, it became clear that the best form for the book, in the circumstance --- and one has to take the latter into account, in these matters – is, a book of 200 photos only --- entirely without your or my comments . . . In short, photos and no text at all. I need scarcely say that I like nothing better than to have you as my editor, and I feel – having seen their book, and read their letters – that we should save our collaboration for another

40. Possibly this would be 'Woodwind Song', one of the last works produced in collaboration with Maxwell Allan, though its material is in fact slate.

project. Instead the book should be the photographer's, worked out with me as regards order and subject . . . and I have written proposing this. I have not yet had a reply. The book they sent, consists entirely of full-page photos of a lady's bottom (or perhaps no lady would allow her bottom to be so used) – of a lassie's bottom, in innumerable situations . . . indeed, in far more situations than anyone but a German could have supposed a lassie's bottom might get into . . All this is very tedious, but given the same space, I think one might do via photos what I had hoped to do in the film . . . (which has been sacrificed to Scotch stupidity). I have therefore given up all thought of a true 'Selected' and want to do something else, something that is obviously a book of photos, of my poems . . . and we will keep our collaboration up our sleeve – I feel the moment will come. Meanwhile I am waiting to hear from the publisher, and am getting a wee bit impatient at the delay. The new photographer lassie promises to be very helpful and nice – we are also contemplating an 'Alphabet Book' for a publisher in New York (for children, that is).

Now Stephen, we are still having an awful financial crisis, which is nothing but the result of my working – and of course I must work when I can, because I am not going to live forever. It is not a kind of near-ish crisis, but is here, and I do feel, very strongly, that my not selling work at high prices, is just an accident, in that no-one actually thinks of buying my things (partly because I'm at Stonypath and not around on The Scene – thank Heaven). It is curious to be both quite famous and entirely neglected, and I think it is probably assumed that I do sell, and have no financial worries. To put it another way, the day will come when it will be considered very stupid that I had to refrain from doing screen prints or glass poems, for lack of cash. Could you, therefore, Stephen, when you are writing people (such as Mr Karpel or R. Motherwell) make a point of speaking about my work and reminding them that I am here. I do not mean that you are to remind them that I am impoverished, but that you could remind them how astonishing it is, that my beautiful prints, or sundials (etc.) are not represented in the Museum of Modern Art, the Tate, or anywhere much at all . . . I specially and sincerely and hopefully ask you to make a point of this, because I think there is a distinction between essential (as it were) neglect, and mere accident. I mean, I'm sure my work should sell: it is pretty well the best of its kind. Naturally I do not like to bother you with this matter, but it is quite serious and real. I am perplexed. I do my best to be practical but I am just not very good at being a business-man.

I hear that the James Laughlin "New Directions Annual", with the photos of my work in it, is out now (though it hasn't arrived here yet).[41] Perhaps because of this, I had a letter from an American publisher of poetry, asking me for an ms. I replied with an interim letter, asking if they had any interest in my booklet-type poems – and putting forward as an immediate suggestion, the idea of your editing a poem/print anthology – I went into this in some detail. I reckon they should just have had my letter and I will let you know what they reply.

I have 2 new poem/prints for you but shant send them till I am sure you are back in Canterbury. Meanwhile I am sending 'Lemons',[42] which I am jolly pleased with . . . Do tell me if you like it. I think it is a triumph, really, if one considers all that might have gone wrong, in the conversion of the little heap of drawings (etc.) – on mere, thin tracing-paper – into the folded concertina (which, incidentally, I am sticking together myself – having let myself in for one-thousand, three-hundred sticks, if I calculate correctly).

Did I tell you that there is now a little cast-iron '**KY**', painted orange – it is very pretty!

And I have done a poem/print with a person who the printer referred to as "the famous Demarco".[43] It was actually the easiest collaboration I have ever been involved in, as The Famous Demarco arranged a day, and hour, with me, drove out with a pretty young lassie, listened to my explanations, looked at my rough sketches and reference materials, and set to work. The rough version was finished before lunch; after lunch, the pretty lassie was ordered to mix the colours; by three.thirty the drawing was complete, and we all went a short walk to sail the protype [sic] of the boat, in the poem/print. It sailed very nicely. And the Famous Demarco left (with lassie), and I packed the print (art-work) for the printer . . . If only Maxwell Allan and John Furnival would be a wee bit like that . . .

This print, by the way, is a fascinating variation on

41. *New Directions* 22 (New York, 1970) had a cover image, and sixteen further plates representing Finlay's work, by the Scottish photographer Ronald Gunn (see also *Midway*, p. 405).

42. *Rhymes for Lemons*, with Margot Sandeman, hand-writing by Gordon Huntly, 1970.

43. *The Little Seamstress*, with Richard Demarco, 1970.

sea ms
sea ms[44]

– I hope it will be ready in a few weeks from now.

So here I will stop. I seem to be awfully busy. It really was splendid to hear from you. I hope you are safely home.

Love,

Ian

PS Did you ever get those two postcards I sent you? (Rip-Tide Sail, and the Fishing News one . .)[45]

P2S *Ocean [Stripe] 5* is again supposed to be made into a film – and maybe it will be . . . .

Canterbury
26 April 1970

Dear Ian,

I have really quite a shoal of poems to thank you for, in addition to your most welcome letter. Indeed I did receive Rip-Tide sail & the Metamorphoses card. They are both splendid – the latter with its ghostly and mysterious grey hue & the former with its boldly pronounced red.

Next in the group is *Rhymes for Lemons*, which Simon [Cutts] had prepared me for in a previous letter. It is a great success – the concertina form, the relation of drawing to writing. I interpret the poetic structure more or less in this way – as the boat(s) is to the lemon(s) (relation of metaphor or rhyme), so the boat's name is to the name as name. In other words, just as the lemon form rhymes with the boat, so the name divides into two 'rhyming' terms –

44. *Seams*, 1969 was a concrete poem/print involving the repeated letters of the one word in a descending column, while *The Little Seamstress* featured the image of a boat sailing (sewing) across the water.

45. *Rip-Tide Sail*, sent 6 March 1970, and *From 'The Metamorphoses of Fishing News'*, sent 26 February 1970, had arrived promptly. See also following letter.

by virtue of its original or proper context & its application to the boat. It is a very beautiful and subtle poem.

Then the 'Sheaves' – it is quite simply the best example I have seen of the equivalence between the poem as object to be explored & the poem as image or conjunction of images.[46] The structure, the superb lettering, the genitive sequence, the land/sea metaphor – all these levels are so exactly interfused. Quite a triumph.

Then the Skylarks: I won't trespass upon its meaning, but it is yet another example of concentration within separate discontinuous terms of a poetic field that is as wide as the skylark's sky (& as whole).[47]

An aesthetic of discontinuity – as I told my students at Venice – that is what we are left with, which would be a sad thing – if the discontinuity were not followed by a 'kind of rehabilitation'.[48]

It's a pity about the Germanic posteriors, & I hasten to conclude that the German firm may not be profitably entrusted with a Selected. But that is good news about the prospect in America, & I hope the idea of a gigantic comprehensive (photos – booklet-type sequences etc.) Selected will soon come to fruition. I suppose I might have another go at Studio Vista, who hesitated before overwhelmed as they were by the productions of Mrs Berjouwi Basrounian Bowler. They seem to want me to do something else, but are leaving the ideas to me.

I am covered with confusion when I realise that you haven't yet seen my *Experimental Painting* book, which came out just before I left for Venice.[49] I must remedy that, though at the moment I am left with one copy only. Reactions from friends and acquaintances have been good, but there has been silence in the world of newspapers.

Very soon I shall be sending my last batch of stuff to Viking for the *Constructivism* book, & I shall take good care to mention and commend your

46. *Sheaves*, folding card, screen print, 1970.

47. *Skylarks*, folding card in envelope: in later correspondence, this poem becomes a key work in our discussions (pp. 66–7, 69), and it features prominently in my essay, 'Ian Hamilton Finlay: Engineer and Bricoleur'.

48. Quoted from Finlay's *Ocean Stripe 5*.

49. *Experimental Painting: Construction, Abstraction, Destruction, Reduction* (London: Studio Vista, 1970).

prints to Mr Karpel. I feel just as you do, on the point of the neglect being accidental. It is a stupid situation, &, one hopes, might change quite suddenly as a result of some circumstance. Thank Sue for her letter with the new list. I shall show it to the people who order English books for our Library – but I feel more is likely to be achieved by getting orders from friends – in any case it is useful to have the new list.

Jim Ede's collection & extension is being opened a week on Tuesday by the Prince of Wales. What a pity the column poem could not be there already! But I'll be able to explain to Jim what the position is.

On regal subjects – can I presume that your inversion of the Declaration of Arbroath is the result of strongly held principle?[50] Ever since I got a letter from [Robert] Pinget with the Gallic cock neatly upside down, I have pondered on the significance of his act, & reached no conclusion –

Is the famous Demarco Hugo Demarco – of black light fame?

All the best to Sue, Eck & Ailie,
Yours

Stephen

Stonypath
2 May 1970

Dear Stephen,

thank you for your most welcome letter. It is always so cheering to hear from you.

I am so glad you like the various things I have sent you recently. I think it would be fair to say that J. Willett's notion that only [Dieter] Rot and Hansjorg [Mayer], have standards, is —- well, peculiar.

I am going to send you some new poem/prints too. The parcelling is all that stands between you and them – if one excludes the GPO. (The sense and the grammar of this sentence are suspect, but you will see what I mean).

50.The Declaration of Arbroath, dated 1320, was sent to Pope John XXII in order to affirm Scotland's status as an independent sovereign state.

No, the famous Demarco is Richard, of the Richard Demarco Gallery. I hope to have that print in the very near future.

I'm delighted that you understand the position with the German publisher. It's a case of giving them something they seem capable of doing. I had a wee note the other day, saying that they are drawing up a contract in the terms I suggested – that the book should be all photos, and that the photographer should share equally in any royalty. (I never mentioned it, but they didn't seem to want to offer you any share in the royalty at all). I have too great a respect for your talents, to involve you willingly in a situation which would be less than perfect in its potential. It is not folly to hope that a 300 page book of photos, sans any text, could be exciting and good; whereas a 'Selected' where the publisher tended to regard the editor as a bit superfluous, would be wrong from the start.

Nothing else has happened about any other 'Selected'. If you could put some suggestion to Studio Vista, about a you/me (us) collaboration, I would be awfully pleased. In case it might help, I enclose, on loan, (since I can't afford to buy more) a copy of the just-out N[ew] D[epartures] Annual, with the photo section. Studio V. might be interested to see this. As you know, there is a feeling in a lot of what are called 'quarters', against exposition and comment; but a long philosophical treatise by you, in which my works figured as illustrations of my argument, would please me very much. And I would be glad to collaborate on helping with suitable 'quotations' too. (If spare copies of other recent things would be useful, you need only say). What I am trying to say here is, that the German publisher was unexcited by the idea of a lengthy essay, and this is a fairly common attitude in certain quarters, whereas – so long as the essay is yours, I mean – I would be entirely delighted to allow my works to figure merely as illustrations in a book which is predominantly an exposition of an aesthetic stance. (I think you will understand this distinction between two kinds of book). I am not of course meaning that the stance in question should be 'mine' – that it would be yours would be the point, and the works would be there because our attitudes converge.

No, if I stuck the Declaration of Arbroath stamp on, upside-down, it was the merest chance. It is a quite noble Declaration, and I'm afraid it could be said that it has not been lived up to . . . Rather tritely, the Flame of Independence which was kindled on the occassion (spelling?) first set fire to its stand, and then went out.

I am delighted to hear about Jim Ede and the Prince of Wales. How sad that Alfred Wallis could not be there.

Derek (Stanford) had mentioned your Experimental Painting book. I would indeed be delighted to see it.

MacMillan (NY) have asked me to do an Alphabet Book for children, (expecting, I suppose, a kind of topsyturvy concrete poem), and I have suggested – with samples – a little book combining plain statements of fact, with photos of various toys and models (all made by me, of course). The new photographer, the lassie, took 3 samples, Glider, Barge, and Motor Fishing Vessel, and the result is superb. I don't [see] how any publisher could resist the idea! --- But publishers have been known to resist my ideas, and we will have to wait and see . . . .[51]

[. . .]

I wonder if you liked the little Waterlily postcard which you (I hope) had from me recently.[52] I plan to have this done as a stone poem, and little stone (formal) pond, in the garden – with an arbour of cypress trees surrounding it. And of course a lily in the water. It could be very pleasing. Essentially, no matter how much work we put into the garden here, it would remain basically a cottage garden: and so poems have to take the form of – as it were – integrated incidents, as opposed to monuments. This is not of course a drawback: limitations are rarely drawbacks if one can contrive to work in harmony with them.

I should shortly have another (very) little garden poem, which is being prepared for me by the engraver in The Botanic Gardens, Glasgow, (by courtesy of the Corporation of that city). This is to take the form of a name-tag, which will stand in our new shrub-bed, at the base of a little tree – a one-word poem; thus:

A Pinnate Evergreen

sea

51. This project would result not in a book of photographs by Diane Tammes as suggested here, but in a selection of concrete poems, printed on coloured papers with inventive new layouts: *Poems to hear and see* (New York: Macmillan, 1971).

52. See the following letter.

– if you have a Chambers Dictionary to hand, you might like to look up the word 'pinnate'.

Well, it was jolly nice to hear from you, Stephen. I hope everything is going well.

Love,

Ian

Canterbury
23 May [1970]

Dear Ian,

Many thanks for your letter & of course for the poem-prints. I am most delighted with the majestic counterpart to *Xmas Star*, & I also like the sea/ms, which *Rip-tide Sail* had in a sense prepared me for. I am highly dubious about the *Catamarangue*, but I expect it is not intended to arouse sentiments of profound trust – in all seriousness (!) I would acclaim its faultless unity of style.[53] Yes, the *Lily Pool* did arrive, & I could easily visualise it in the kind of natural setting which you mention.

The *New Directions* selection is most effective. I have sent it off to Studio Vista & am awaiting a reply. The irony is that they are for ever asking me to do, or to recommend a doer for, a companion volume to *Experimental Painting* on *Experimental Sculpture*. But I explain that somehow it doesn't apply in the same way (& anyhow it has been done, in a more or less satisfactory way). It is much more difficult to imagine how to convince them of a valuable but novel project than to fall in with what is really an unnecessary complement to a series. (By the way, a copy of *Exp.p.* should be arriving at Stonypath before long).

I got a letter from Sunderland asking for works to exhibit, a catalogue preface & an essay for your exhibition all at the same time. It rather took my breath away! I am inclined to suggest that I just do the essay (which they apparently

53. Finlay had posted in a roll his most recent prints: *Seams* (usually, but perhaps wrongly, dated 1969), *Poem/Print No. 14 ('Xmas Rose')* and *Catameringue* (both dated 1970); the card, *A Waterlily Pool*, had been posted on 10 April.

want to be quite long).[54] There is so little interest in trying to draw an ungainly circle around a motley collection of English concrete poets (I note the fate of poor Frank Popper, who gets into terrible tangles trying to write connected pieces in which everyone's mite is featured), But I may be overestimating the breadth of the exhibition.

The past few weeks have been the occasion of sundry expeditions & enterprises. The expedition to Cambridge was very successful, with a magnificent concert & Jim [Ede] being splendidly natural and unaffected among the dignitaries. Ron Costley was there (he has a habit of appearing on these occasions!) & I congratulated him on the lettering for SHEAVES.

Second came the expedition to Paris, where I was directing the faltering steps of a group of M.A. students & a professor. We had a memorable morning at the Matisse exhibition, which was prolonged well into the afternoon. The French have done supremely well in their new arrangement of the Grand Palais, which allows you to take a delicious meal between sections of the exhibition. I have been used to feeling somewhat ethereal in the last rooms of major ventures of this kind. But in this case, renewed vigour helped us to see the later papiers peints, and the big pictures from Russia, at their best.

This enterprise was followed by one on home ground: a Structuralist Symposium at Canterbury, to which various contributors to *20th Century Studies* were summoned. I think it advanced us very slightly along the paths of knowledge and truth . . .[55]

Finally came my trip to Nottingham, at the beginning of this week. I stayed with Simon [Cutts] & Stuart [Mills] came to dinner in the evening. The ostensible occasion was a lecture on 'Classicism' (as an aspect of Neo-Classicism, Synthetism, Constructivism & Structuralism).[56] I think it was quite successful, although I was quite aware that my approach was not wholly congenial to any member of the audience except Simon. I seem to

54. This request from the Ceolfrith Gallery at Sunderland was to be the origin of my essay, 'Ian Hamilton Finlay: Engineer and Bricoleur'. See pp. 92–3.

55. The symposium was held at Rutherford College, to mark the publication of *20th Century Studies* 3 (May 1970) on Structuralism, and featured as speakers present and future contributors to the journal such as Roger Poole, Geoffrey Nowell-Smith and the Editor, Guido Almansi. The artist Anthony Hill, who had contributed an article on 'A Structuralist Art?' to this issue, also attended.

56. My letter of invitation from the Principal of the Nottingham College of Art and Design proposed the title 'Some Aspect of Classicism'.

have delighted him by telling one of the staff that Robert Morris' minimal sculptures are really gestural painting.

Simon is designing an invitation for a Satie/Cage concert that I am sponsoring at the end of June. A pianist & a soprano will be coming from Paris, & a number of most effective songs (such as those from Léon-Paul Fargue's *Ludions*) will be performed.[57]

Oh dear – I haven't looked up 'pinnate' yet – does it have to be a Chamber's Dictionary?

I must close now, as the Bank Holiday will obviously cause great interruptions in the post if I don't get this letter in beforehand.

Love to Sue, Eck & Ailie
Yours

Stephen

Stonypath
3 June 1970

Dear Stephen,

how nice it was to have your letter (23 May) as it always is: you are great at the letters (as I'm sure Harry Lauder once put it) --- when I see your handwriting on the envelope I get a lovely feeling of anticipation almost entirely untinged with apprehension (which is very rare in my case, for who knows what horrors a post may hold!)

We have had a very hot day – perhaps **THE** hot day, rather like the latter part of the day you were last here (preceding that lurid pink dawn, that yoghurt-carton-coloured thunderous 6 a.m.). What with The World Cup, and innumerable visitors, and a new lawn-mower we have acquired, the world seems quite holidayish and upsidedown.

57. The concert took place as planned at the end of June. The soprano Aline Dallier (wife of Frank Popper) was accompanied by a stylish black pianist, Andres Wheatley, and both performed songs and piano pieces by Erik Satie, including those after poems by Léon-Paul Fargue. The second half of the concert was a piece entitled 'Surindeterminacy', which Aline Dallier had adapted from the music and writings of John Cage.

I'm glad the poem/prints reached you. I will shortly send you the true sequel to 'seams', the one I've done with the Richard Demarco of the Richard Demarco Gallery (Richard Demarco Street, Richard Demarco – one of the few countries not competing in The World Cup?). He is just wee Richard Demarco, not the one you mention, (who is unknown to me). Anyway it is a **SUPERB** print: it is a **CLASSIC**. (As a matter of fact, all my recent things are classics, it is quite pleasing).

I wonder what Studio Vista will make of the New Directions feature. I was thinking that it would be **JUST** like the thing, if I have no sooner signed the contract with the German publisher, than SV decide they would not do the book of your criticism (essay) with my things, but would do a straight book on my things.*[*i.e. by you]. I mean, the situation would be familiar. So maybe you could discretely advise them that I am about to sign a contract with the German firm and they (SV) must act now if they are going to because being sad afterwards will do no good at all . . . And I will sign the German contract unless it's positively Wagnerian, for the photographer is (as they say) raring to go.

Did I tell you that I am having a formal lilypool built? Oh yes I did. But did I tell you the 'Bowl of Ahaz' type Sundial is --- at long last --- almost complete (Maxwell Allan tells me)?[58] And the SCOTTISH ZULU print is at the screenprinter![59] I am of course going to send a presentation copy to Enoch Powell.

About Sunderland. There is – was? – a mixed show of British Concrete, which I declined to be in (and found Stuart had entered!). Then I am having a one-man show there in the autumn, of prints and photos. It is for this that your essay was requested, I am sure. Now Stephen, the gallery/shop asked me to ask you, and I replied that, as I supposed they weren't paying you, it seemed an awfully big thing to ask you to do . . . and that, while there was no-one I would rather be written about by, I hadn't the heart to ask you on their behalf. They now seem to have asked you, and the demand still feels excessive, and what I wonder is, if you couldn't arrange with the gallery to be allowed to place [it] in America or somewhere, the same text, and get paid for it? I do

58. A bowl-shaped sundial, containing water, whose design follows the Renaissance recreation of an apparatus mentioned in the Book of Isaiah.

59. *Scottish Zulu*, screenprint with David Button, 1970.

worry about being a demand or drag, and at least I can make it clear that I realise how much work is involved ---- and I hope I have managed to make my appreciation of your writing, very clear indeed.

If there is anything that is still obscure in the situation, let's get it sorted out. You are too valuable to be taken for granted.

I am **FASCINATED** to hear about your Satie concert. I suppose you would refuse to perform my interpretation of the Morsels of a Pear, punctuated (at artistic intervals) by the BBC pips? (The work is entitled, Happy Satie Pip).

Tut Tut Tut Tut Tut.

I hope the Pinnate Soprano is a great success.

Fancy you lecturing at Simon's Art College! The students would (of course) be ignorant but were they also mutinous?

Yesterday we had a nice visit from Nigel Gosling, who (I am told) is the Art Critic of The Observer. As a matter of fact, Richard Demarco brought him (so I reckon that proves that R. Demarco is not in The World Cup). How my heart sank at the onset of another London one . . . and how it rose when Nigel turned out to be a delightful, elderly, courteous, civilised Englishman of the nicest kind! Really, it was a most pleasant visit. Unlike most London ones, he was interested in everything from the sheep, to the weeds, to the little submarine which I am building from plywood (for Mr Kenedy at the V & A, I believe you know him?) . . . He even looked at my poems. And he gave a great impression of being pleased to be here, and even asked if he might come again with his wife . . Altogether a delightful surprise. Have you perhaps met NG, Stephen? He was really so un-ignorant and un-mutinous as to be entirely heart-warming. How nice nice people are! And he never **ONCE** said **MONEY** or **PUBLIC IMAGE** or **DAVID HOCKNEY** (unlike a London one who was here the day **BEFORE**, said he darkly, and took a lot of photos with what he said was David Hockney's camera, a frightful thought – Heaven knows **WHERE** I will be developed and <u>who with</u> . . .)

Richard Demarco (of Richard Demarco fame) has done the drawing for my 'Glossary', which is the sequel to 'Errata', which Ron Costly [sic] **OUGHT** to be printing about **NOW**. Glossary will of course be dedicated to Hugh MacDiarmid, and Errata to Stuart Montgomery.

Now I must stop. Write soon, Love,

Aye,

Ian

P.S. Stephen, I <u>know</u> it is a bore, but I am still <u>awfully</u> worried about not selling my things and I am just entirely hopeless about knowing what to do. I suppose I should <u>ask</u> ones like Nigel Gosling, frankly: but it somehow seems impolite – and then, people just <u>assume</u> that I sell my work without any trouble. Do you think you could perhaps give an evening to writing letters (to the Museum of Modern Art, etc), saying about my prints and so on. It is too <u>silly</u> to have cupboards full of beautiful prints which every gallery <u>ought</u> to have . . . And then there are the postcards and books, too – not to mention the stone poems. I am quite <u>perplexed</u> about being so famous and neglected. Please forgive my writing all this – I <u>know</u> how busy you are.

PPS I am looking forward <u>very</u> much to seeing the Experimental Painting book.

Stonypath
9 June 1970

Dear Stephen,

this is a wee extra letter, to thank you for your Studio Vista book which has arrived, and has been a <u>great excitement</u> for me. Naturally I am pleased to be there – and I am very pleased and proud to see what my old friend Stephen can do: <u>I do congratulate you</u>. I have not of course read the book all through yet, as I must finish a book I am presently reading (on Chinese philosophy) – but I have dipped about and enjoyed the dippings ----- I hadn't quite realised that the book was so much a serious essay (as opposed to a 'survey'), and the former category is so much more interesting.*[* It was very kind of you to send me the book, Stephen.]

It also made me wish that you were within chatting distance, for I had – have – a great urge to take up the bit in your last letter where you say that Studio Vista might consider companion volumes . . . Couldn't you suggest one on concrete poetry, and do, not a survey, but (say) three long essays, one on me, one on [Eugen] Gomringer, and one on someone else . . . (??) What I would say to you, if you were here ---- letters have such a weight that one hesitates to say things that might seem pushing – is, that another survey of concrete would be superfluous, but I (at least) am horrified at the continuing lack of definition – critical categories – for what I am doing (which is not, after all – and how could it be – what I was doing a few years ago). I was horrified to find that even Simon [Cutts] (a bright chap if ever there was one) seemed to entirely miss the point of 'Skylarks' – missing the point being something different from simply not liking it.

Now, if I may dwell on that wee work a moment, I am perfectly aware that it is not Guernica (no, it's a jolly sight better: joke), so that when I want to dwell on it, it is not because I'm making any assumption of importance. But there is the question of method, and it's here that I feel an increasing – indeed yawning – gulf which was not there between poet and reader in straightforward (!) concrete. For instance, Simon seems to have thought the thing was about Skylarks – which it is, of course – but it is really a poem which depends on a system of references to other works of art, and other methods, if it is to be enjoyed.

Thus: it is a sentimental Greetings Card. And it certainly is that. And may be enjoyed as such. But there is an area of culture in which a Skylark is certainly a boat, in the way that Fido is a dog, and I am expecting the reader to know that and to take it as a 'given'. Well now, if we consider the large part that yachts play in the wee drawing, and how far-off the birds are, and if we consider how much the sentence is about actual Skylarks (birds), we have a kind of hovering ambiguity in the whole, which really functions like a distancing irony. And we have to realise that the words – which are a direct quotation from a well-known treatise on birds – are present in exactly the way that Schwitters' bus-ticket is present --- they are collage, and the pleasure is, that something as accurate (as it were) as a bus-ticket* [* the drawing itself is a collage, of 2 drawings, the far-off bird being an addition to the original] is capable of being simultaneously and without strain, a metaphor relating to the yachts --- yachts being things which, you will remember, feature quite largely in French Symbolist poetry* [*as well as in the painters of the time]. (Mallarmé sailed one) . . . and which (in a prepared context) we can surely understand as ground birds . . . with aerial songs --- in fact, with sails. A prosaic and factual sentence has here become something quite else, while remaining itself.

Now, this image is (I think) a very satisfactory one – and I see no reason why the reader can't take it further, and see that if the birds are a metaphor for the boats, the boats may be a metaphor for something else, the whole notion of Beauty and Freedom. But all this is only possible if the reader will grant (as he would certainly grant had the poem been an obviously literary product) that a work of art can draw on different areas of culture as well as on the external world. And the difficulty (or one of them) lies in the fact that the poem draws on several worlds, areas of culture, which are usually regarded as incompatible – the area where dogs are Fido and yachts are Skylarks, and the area where a bus ticket may be an abstract rectangle of colour, and the area of the Symbolists . . and so on. (The reader should also be familiar with Shelley and Wordsworth). I fully agree that my manner of expounding this, is awful: but the method is a reasonable artistic one, and it ought to be understood, available, there. Of course I have stressed the 'cultural reference' aspect, but there is equally a reference to the 'real' world, the beautiful yachts. I think it would be fair to say that something is said about the beauty of the yachts* which could not be said so purely and resonantly in another way (at this moment in time). [*that their sails in the air are like songs – (an image which is at once very traditional and a bit daring) – that they (prose wont complete this) . . . .]

Now all this – which I have so crudely expounded – is to me axiomatic. But I also see that the whole method – so clear to me – is lost on other people, who are at another chapter in the universal book. And this is very perplexing. Anyone who doubts this, should try to write a sonnet, imagining an audience which has no conception of the form – which is used, say, to the heroic couplet and nothing else.

I have gone on about this wee poem because it's a good example of how far my wee boat (The Skylark?) is from the quay where the reader – even Simon as reader – stands. (I am of course aware that Simon may have been busy and just not bothered to think about the poem at all, but the general point stands).

Now I will just stop, as my prose depresses me awfully, and gives me a headache. (Your prose is another matter).

Love,

Ian

Canterbury
Tuesday 16 June [1970]

Dear Ian,

I was delighted to get both your letters, the learned postcard & the beautiful 'Little Seamstress'.[60] Holding my reactions to the two latter in reserve, I shall begin by saying that I had just written – on the very point of receiving your first letter – to two possibly productive outlets for your work: the London Graphic Arts Gallery and Bernard Karpel. In the first case, I am more than a little chary, as the LGA people are rather frighteningly on the make & even tried at one point (with supreme audacity or was it ignorance?) to steal Vasarely from Denise René.[61] But that is in some ways to the good, as they appear to have most effective selling power. I received a tentative letter from them in reply, which left a possibility of their advancing further.

As for B. Karpel – I wrote at length about your difficulties being in the nature of post-modernist things, & implied, I hope, that such a body as the Museum of Modern Art should be pre-eminently devoted to spotting the kind of work which transgressed the ancestral categories.

I am still keeping on at Studio Vista, which is rather like a soft * *

*

(postponement of letter owing to succession of end of term crises – scribe resumes Saturday 20 June)

Studio Vista have just replied – & I am afraid they consider that the book, though an 'interesting' prospect, would be of too little selling power at present. At the same time, they do refer to your original suggestion, for a book of poem-prints as something that 'seems to have fallen through' owing to Robin Wright's withdrawal to ponder his soul on the isle of Skye (yes –). I wonder if that means they are still interested?

60. I had already been informed of Richard Demarco's highly efficient collaboration on the screen print of 'The Little Seamstress' (see p. 54). The 'learned postcard' was *Still Life with Lemon* (sent to me on 10 June 1970). This work had its title translated into French and German on the reverse of the card, thus recalling the titles of Modernist still-life paintings.

61. From the 1950s onwards, Vasarely had been the mainstay of the Denise René Gallery, Paris, then the leading French centre for kinetic art.

They ask me if I know anyone who would be qualified to do a complete book of Gauguin's graphic work – the prospect is a gloriously tempting one, & I am almost disposed to make myself a Gauguin scholar for the purpose!

Incidentally, Ian, you have a glorious, equally glorious surprise in store for the beginning of August. Not to unveil the secret too excessively, I should say that my visit to a Parisian exhibition not unconnected with an artist who goes under the initials 'M.D.' will at that time be bearing fruit in the way of lavish catalogues[62] –

It was a great pleasure to hear that you had received, & were initially pleased with the Experimental Painting book. Yes, it is far from a survey, that being a dismal way of going about any such subject. I am really quite pleased with the 'prise de position' it represents, though I know it will appeal to fairly few people. Frank Malina wrote to me that as a 'practising artist' (verb.sap.) he could not approve of my efforts.

To come to the 'Little Seamstress' & the card: both seem to move so centrally in the Symbolist/Synthetist world. In fact I think 'Little Seamstress' is really one of the very finest picture/poems that you have done. That colour (chosen by R.D. & mixed by the girl, if I remember rightly) is something hardly seen in Western Art since Fauvism – or indeed before Post-Impressionism.

I must start to think about my essay for the Sunderland people – it is a good idea to suggest that I do it while reserving rights to further publication. I had suggested that a good way of securing the right quid pro quo would be if they paid for me to visit Stonypath (from Yorkshire). Let's see what they think.

I quite understand your worry about 'Skylarks' & audience reactions to it. This is the kind of problem that I would like to deal with when I write my article – partly the anthropological (Lévi-Strauss) notion of 'bricolage' (as in *Form* 2),[63] & partly the idea of Classicism depending on both a primary and a secondary code or coded series (the primary code being formal, the secondary one cultural: all interest lies in the parallel phasing of the two).

62. Finlay had long been intent in acquiring a book or catalogue that featured the paintings of the French Synthetist artist Maurice Denis (see *Midway*, p. 340). The opportunity of an exhibition at the Grand Palais enabled me to purchase such a catalogue (though hardly a 'lavish' one) on his behalf. See pp. 89–90, 93.

63. The reference is to the essay by the Italian critic Gillo Dorfles, 'For and against a Structuralist Aesthetic!', which Philip Steadman and I translated for *Form* 2 (September, 1966).

Of course you are right in saying that your work has changed immeasurably over the last year or two. That is the thing that must be properly understood & appreciated. But how hard to convince any moderately concerned spectator of the art world that an artist can undertake to rehabilitate what is public – rather than maintain the illusion that he is purveying the private.

My concert approaches – it is liberally scattered with songs from poems by Léon-Paul Fargue –

Love to Sue, Eck and Ailie
Yours

Stephen

Stonypath
29 June 1970

Dear Stephen,

how nice it was – as always – to have your letter . . . and right in the middle of the soaprano season. [sic] The bit about 'M D' and the glorious August surprise, is all too tantalising. Martha Doto?[64] MacDiarmid? Ah well, one had best leave Time with a few surprises up his sleeve.

Frank Malina's description of himself as a 'practising artist', (when delivering his comments on your book), remind[s] one of the well-known saying, Practice makes Perfect. In his case, this might be amended to, Practice may make less imperfect . . . And the practice I would recommend is, that he should copy the Old Masters for 8 hours a day, for the next 3 years. Your book is jolly good. You must sometimes get a bit depressed by the amount of idiocy that surrounds you.

That is disappointing about Studio Vista. Perhaps you should poke them, once more, on the subject of the poem/print book, since they seem to have at least remembered the idea. Isn't it extraordinary how unadventurous this age is, while seeing itself as the very essence of Artistic Polar Exploration? (Sorry, Planetary: I reveal my upbringing). It was nice of you to write to B. Karpel, and in fact I heard from him . . . a small order, and clipped arrogant note,

64. *Alias* Martha Boto (kinetic artist featured in *Image*, 1964).

which aroused my ire.* [*and caused a sense of **FUTILITY**] He has ordered 3 of the prints, the out-of-print ones, at £5 each – the very ones he refused to buy, a few years ago, when they cost five shillings. Then, with great daring, he has ordered one of my own, a recent one, the Xmas Star. Bloody hell. I am very tempted just to send the [Franz] Mon and [Ferdinand] Kriwet and whatever the other one was, together with a curt note saying that there would be no point in them having only one of my recent prints, since it would be entirely incomprehensible out of the context of my work*. [***SHALL** do this, I think] And this is true. It is really very depressing. The possibility of being understood, seems to get further and further away.

I was reminded of this the other day, when Robert Nye invited me to send poems for The Scotsman. I just felt that there was a total lack of point in offering recent poems to an audience which would not only be hostile, but would be totally ill-informed. The irony is, that concrete poems of the ten-years-ago (or whatever it was) sort, seem to be what's expected of me now . . . and the Scottish Arts Council even turned down (very politely) the poster I did for them, with a long explanation which made it clear that they had been expecting me to do a 'concrete' poem! Anyway, I just told Robert Nye, (you know, politely) that there was no point at all in sending my recent poems. It is not that they are examples of giant complexity, but no one in their senses is going to offer to play lawn tennis in the middle of a football-anticipating crowd in Hampden Park.

The 'True Vine' sundial is now in place, and must be the only (?) sundial in the world, which is rigged with net-rope, and is adjusted (at the gnomon) by a bowsie! The new lilypool is also in place, and is settling down (ominous phrase to use of a pool) after an initial crisis caused by a leak. Seen down the length of the lawn, it offers a very pleasantly classical silhouette, interrupted by a branch of a cypress tree.

The Land/Sea Sundials are coming along, after a whole series of criseses [sic]. First, the cardboard idea had to be abandoned, as the warping (in the windowsill heat) would be excessive. I now have a glass version suitable for use on a balcony or indoor/outdoor area --- or (of course) by anyone who has a South-facing windowsill and a zeppelin (on which to ride around to the outside of the window when they want to read the time). I am now carrying this dial to stage 2, which has the lettering reversed, so that the shadow is read from the reverse side. It is all very complicated, since the sun has a direction, its shadows have 2 directions (morning and night), letters have one direction, and people don't hang out of windows by their fingertips to read indoor sundials. I am, however, pleased with progress so far. I am also doing a horizontal version in aluminium. Your little prose piece is going to be invaluable.

I am reading a **FIRST-RATE** – almost as intelligent as my dear Stephen – book by one Edward Hyams, on gardens.[65] I always knew this book must exist and now I have found it. (At one time I feared it would not exist until you wrote it). This book understands perfectly, that a garden ought to be a work of **ART** (I would not claim that **MINE** even begins to be); and it also understands – how nice – that 'There is only one art . .', and that the idea that X or Y, who engaged in various modes of art, were minor because they disippated (spelling?) their talents, is **NONSENSE**. Rather, they were minor because they were minor, and that is all. (Not that I think there's anything wrong with minor art). This, as you will see, shows up the fallacy of the **BETWEEN** poetry and painting idea. Anyway, such erudition and sensibility are rare --- and **VERY** rare in Englishmen who write in the [New] Statesman (as E Hyams used to do, I remember. And maybe does). More of this excellent book later.

I am at present nursing (as they say) a bruised leg, and am a hobbledehoy. Nothing would content Mr Finlay but that he embarked in his sailing dinghy (the **IOTA**) in a gale. Alas, the wind catching the sail, the tiller-bar was thrown violently sideways, and he (who had thought to find safety on the floor of his vessel, rather than on the lofty eminence of the exposed seat), was first tumbled on his back, and then, in a trice, swept clean over the side. Our inland mariner now knows why old-time sailors lashed their tillers in storms.

We are all looking forward to seeing you at Stonypath (sailing into the teeth of gales).

Now I must close and address myself to making the final corrections to the lay-outs of 'A Sailor's Calendar', my 18th century-style Miscellany, which will shortly go to the printer. It promises well. Errata and Glossary are also coming along, and I think they should be exciting. (Any suggestions for further items in this series?)

65. Edward Hyams, *The English Garden*, London: Thames and Hudson, 1964 (paperback edition 1966).

Do write when you can. You are a great encourager, Stephen. Many good wishes, and I hope all goes well on all fronts. I look forward to an account of the soprano. A word which I associate, for some reason, with another word, Ice-cream. Dame Peach Melba, I expect.

Love from all, Aye,

Ian

In my letter of 16 June, I mentioned that I had written to Bernard Karpel, Librarian of the Museum of Modern Art in New York, suggesting that he should buy a large stock of Finlay's works, rather than making the single print order which Finlay mentioned in the previous letter. In his reply to my letter, Karpel announced that he was in fact willing to purchase 'everything', and proposed an advance of $100. I forwarded the new letter to Finlay with the covering note that follows here. In my subsequent reply to Karpel (15 July 1970), I enquired how we were to interpret 'everything', given that Finlay's work involved 'poem/constructions' (such as the poems sand-blasted on glass), as well as printed materials. In reply to me (see letter of 30 June), Finlay suggested sending photographs of his recent works in situ at Stonypath, as well as a full complement of prints and booklets. This decision met with the approval of Karpel (letter to me of 20 July 1970), who however warned me that he had 'no way of knowing what [his] reaction [to the work] might be' (see my letter to Finlay of 4 August).

Canterbury
[late June, 1970]

Dear Ian,

This seems promising, doesn't it? If you would like me to write and suggest the $100 against potential acquisitions, I will do so (he is away until 20 July – so there is a fair amount of time).

From next Tuesday (30 June) I shall be in Huddersfield for the ensuing week. Then to France ultimately on 17 July.

Yours Stephen

Satie concert arriving this evening!

Stonypath
[pm 30 June 1970]

Dear Stephen,

a hasty note, following my letter yesterday, or rather, your letter yesterday enclosing Mr Karpel's.

KARPels in your garden pond or lake
How long time keeps your hearts awake . . . .[66]

It had struck me that his previous, niggardly response was but a coincidence; but I thought it too unlikely! The things now is, that I'm not quite sure what he means by sending

"everything here"

– everything printed?

Perhaps a solution would be, to send a large selection of printed things, plus a large selection of the photos which the new photographer will be taking, of the outdoor (etc) works? I do think the things in a setting are much more persuasive; and along with the printed things, should suggest an "everything".

I feel that, if the offer is there, there is no instant rush. I wonder if you are coming up to see us – perhaps on your return from France? (Travellers do Return from that Dire Bourne?) – At which time I would have the new photos, & we could discuss it ----- and perhaps enclose your new essay too?

Thank you very much, Stephen.

All for now, rushing for Postie.

Aye,

Ian

PS Give our love to your mother, who has a place in our hearts. It's an ignorant and mutinous world.

66. See note 35.

Stonypath
26 July 1970

Dear Stephen,

I hope you would have Sue's letter [19 July], in explanation of my silence.[67] I was – as always – most pleased to hear from you, but was simply too exhausted to reply, (except in my head: I wrote you some very long and brilliant letters there).

I do hope you don't mind your visit being postponed till September. As I think Sue told you, it will give us a wee Hope for the end of Summer. Our mid-Summer visits have really been too much for us this year. Friends are not, of course, tiring – but there are also acquaintances, which are another matter. Some – Mike [Weaver]'s Professor is an example[68] – simply won't take a polite 'No' for an answer . . . and one ends up flattened with nervous exhaustion, and in dire need of Iron Tonics and all that sort of carry-on. So we judged it best to ask both you and Simon – i.e. the two pals we really look forward to seeing – to delay your visits till we recover a bit. And I hope we have learned a lesson and wont get overwhelmed again.

Meanwhile my letters (correspondence) are/is altogether out of control. I am actually – astonishing situation – doing 5 wee books with other publishers, and vital communications have had to be ignored while I sat swathed in rugs, sooking vast lollipops of iron bars and munching filings. This is therefore more of a note than a letter.

No, I have **NOT** heard from the Sunderland people, and the photographer who is to share the show with me (exhibiting a selection of the photos she is now taking for the German publisher's book, provisionally titled 'Ian Hamilton Finlay' – a title it shares with myself), has not heard either, and I am very irked. All their promises of a vast and pretty catalogue, have melted away. Perhaps we should all melt away too?

What I have done, (not reprehensibly, I hope) is to suggest to The Black Sparrow Press that you will write a not too large introduction for 'Honey By

67. Sue's letter, explaining the need to put off my summer visit till September, reached me in the Auvergne, where I was once more staying at the Château de Barante (see *Midway*, p. 136).

68. Reverend Moelwyn Merchant, Professor at the University of Exeter (see also *Midway*, pp. 395, 398).

The Water', my last collection of pure concrete, which contains, in plain classical form, many poems of the last six or so years, which will be familiar to you. As the book is to be American, I felt a corrective introduction was needed; and as I also felt/feel you must be paid, I have suggested that they either manage this themselves or give you a share in my royalty (which wont, alas, be in advance but will eventually exist. They are businesslike, I think.) I would be awfully pleased if you can manage this intro. When it comes to it – which wont be yet.* [*I hope you will hear from them eventually.][69]

(That grammar sounds grotesque but I see no other way of framing the thought.)

(Iron In The Soul).

As soon as Awfully Urgent letters are chalked off, we will think about Mr Karpel. Perhaps I should get the local joiner to construct a flat box, to contain the poem/prints, with a good sprinkling of wee booklets on top of them – like pepper on sauce?

The Stedelijk [Museum, Amsterdam] has asked me to make an outdoor poem for that show they are having, but these requests are always so vague, and vaguely rushed, and the finances so unclear, that it is more of a worry than a pleasure. I will do the best I can.

Meanwhile, there have been various **DISASTERS** in that department, as Maxwell [Allan]'s formal pond turned out to leak, and after it was sorted, it leaked again . . and Maxwell's maddeningly evasive attitude (coupled with the thought that I was being charged £200 or so, for such a teeny pond, which was, in the event, not formal enough to hold water), was too much . . . The pond is now at my gate (where I put it) and I have embarked on what I hope may well prove a more pleasant collaboration with a very well-known carver and designer, Michael Harvey, who stays in Bridport.[70] He is rather august, but I have come to the conclusion, that it had best be the august or nothing,

69. This project eventually proved a great success. *Honey by the Water*, a collection of Finlay's concrete poems from the 1960s, and 'Seven Sundials' from the more recent period, were published in 1973 by the Black Sparrow Press, with my 'Afterword' on 'modern Classicism'. The phrase 'Honey by the water' is taken from a poem by the Irish writer Austin Clarke, entitled 'The Last Heifer'. See also pp. 107, 151.

70. This is Finlay's first reference to the eminent letter-carver who would shortly become one of his important collaborators, bringing a new standard of technical ability and aesthetic finesse to the garden works.

for February and March have let me down . . . Mr Harvey has written very enthusiastically, and I am hopeful that this attempt may prove better* [*In the long-term].

I suppose you haven't seen his work? It is really very superb and totally posh, with a wide range of 'manners'.

Another good bit of news: Ian Proctor, who is a very famous designer of racing yachts and dinghys (and who designed the dinghy we have), has agreed to do a poem/print with me. It is an idea I have had for a long time, but being able to have the boat-plans drawn by the actual designer, is a lovely touch of 'collage'. Moreover, his response to my letter suggests that my idea was one he had long had secretly, which was very pleasing.[71] He is also designing a special sail for our sailboat, so that we can sail in stormy weather. How very distinguished!

Well now, Stephen, please forgive this wee letter all its shortcomings. I will hope to do better next time. I am only just on my feet. It is always **SPLENDID** to hear from you, and we all send our love, and hope you are having a pleasant summer. Aye,

Ian

Clough House
Almondbury
Huddersfield
4 August [19]70

Dear Ian,

I expect that by now you will have got my lethargic postcard which is unlikely to have travelled across France with as great rapidity as myself. Once again, let me say that August is dissolving with such speed – & I am to return to France on 12 August – that a later September visit would seem the ideal and only solution.

It was splendid to get your letter & to learn about the transition from the rugs on to the feet again. I was particularly impressed by the notion of the iron

71. For the fulfilment of this collaboration, see pp. 131–33.

lollipops, since I have been reading Michel Foucault's book on 'The Idea of Folly in the age of Classicism' (to be symmetrically completed by a much needed survey on the 'Idea of Classicism in the age of Folly'?). Here iron is (was) held to have the amazing property of passing directly into the organism without rust or waste – a property which makes it hardly a whit inferior to the 'famous Queen of Hungary water' (liberally taken by Mme de Sévigné as a 'good against sadness').

I hope that by now you are even better, & so able to view with equanimity the enclosed copy of a letter from Bernard Karpel. His phrase about 'having no way of knowing what (his) reaction would be' is redolent, don't you think?

I was delighted with the news of various projects on hand: the 5 books, the Stedelijk possibility, & Ian Proctor. I do hope the Stedelijk comes to something, since I should then have an excellent excuse for crossing over to what is certainly my favourite Modern Art Museum. And I should mention that the garden is a particularly nice feature.

In the absence of signs of life from Sunderland, I am glad that the 'Honey by the Water' collection seems to promise scope for an introductory essay. Any arrangement about payment is suitable for me. I look forward to hearing from them, hopefully on my possible brief Kentish landfall c. 31 August. (I shall then have about a fortnight in Paris researching by day & carousing by night, or so I ideally imagine).

I shall write again, either from Canterbury or from France (where I shall [be] with my parents & so attracted to lake-sides & other places of elegant loitering). Sadly the publication connected with the initials M.D. will not transpire till Sept. But then –

Love to Sue, Eck & Ailie.
Yours

Stephen

Stonypath
4 August [pm 6 August 1970, marked Urgent]

Dear Stephen,

your Man of Iron was delighted to hear from you, the more especially as your summers are now spent like those of the swallow, here, and there. Your 'Idea of Classicism in the Age of Folly', is one of those inventions that make me smile inwardly and outwardly for months. Thank you very much.

We will shortly attend to Bernard Karpel. Heaven knows what he will make of my things.

Ideally, or even practically, I would have delayed this letter till a more energetic moment, (I have spent all today's already), but I have another urgent request. It is a jolly good thing that you are a patient pal.

Also, that you are a credulous pal, and aware that life is often stranger than Scottish Fiction. The situation is this:

You will no doubt be aware that Mr MacDiarmid stays in Biggar, which is 8 miles distant from Stonypath (if one thinks geographically rather than aesthetically). Well:

The Provost of Biggar (of whose existence I was wholly unaware till the other day), came to see me, with the splendid idea that Biggar should mark European Conservation Year, and certain renovations made in its Main Street, by installing a poem of mine. This idea was (needless to say) entirely the Provost's own: he wants it in place by September 4; when it is to be unveiled by Lady Tweedsmuir.

If you are accepting all this so far, I will go on to say, that this is very short notice for any stone/poem, and things were not made easier by my having resolved **NEVER** to work with Maxwell again (for reasons I will go into another time, but they are ultimately aesthetic). Now then, I may have mentioned that I hope to work with Michael Harvey, a very well-known carver and typographer who stays in Bridport (once a home of the merchant fore-and-afters); so I asked MH, and he has been terribly nice about the Biggar stone, and is doing all he can to have it ready in time. The main problem is to get the actual piece of stone, at such short notice, as it is 4ft by 4ft (or rather Biggar than my usual). MH 'phoned tonight to say that he is quite willing to come up here to do the carving, if need be, which is very un-Maxwell of him, and altogether pleasant and generous and nice.

Meanwhile, the Provost also 'phoned, to say that a rival faction of the Council, have erected, or has erected, a fountain on the poem's site – but that he is confident this can be removed to make way for the stone.

So, allowing for the inevitable snags which attend such enterprises, everything is very encouraging.

Now then, Stephen the Provost is a very nice and unexpected kind of chap, and I can well imagine the kind of difficulties he has with his Council, not least in the present matter. So I suggested to him that it might be a suitable assistance to the project, if there was a leaflet which explained the poem, and if this leaflet was kept in the Biggar shops and given to perplexed customers. The Provost thought this was a splendid idea, and said that he could have it printed locally if I could provide the text. I said I thought you might be willing. Do you think, Stephen, you could possibly write a couple of hundred illuminating and diplomatic words, about a poem you have never seen? I would be awfully glad if you could, and I am sure you would, if you only had met the Provost, who is one of those humble and decent souls who hold the world together by wee Dreams of Felicity . . . . It would obviously be an advantage if you could see the poem (as you will, later) but I can perhaps provide enough material to make a basis for your text . . .

(There is certainly enough material for a Scottish novel, but that is another matter).

I will put everything, hopefully, on a separate page.

In haste, and Hope, Love,

Aye,

Ian

The Poem:

Azure & Son
Islands Ltd
Oceans Inc

– This is actually from 'A Sailor's Calendar', my new collection, which Dick Higgins is rumoured to be publishing. It's a nice poem, I think.

Now, (unless the present plan has to be altered), the poem is to be incorporated in a SUNDIAL, and the whole thing will consist of a giant slab, 4ft by 4ft square, by 2 inches (?), which will sit on a round pedastol,* [* by courtesy Simon Cutts] about 3 ft 6, by 12 high.

On the side, or somewhere, in smaller letters, it is to say that the stone was erected in European Conservation Year, a happy handle which ties it into Solar Time).

The site of the poem is a round traffic island in the main street, (which inordinately broad); the island is quite reachable, as it only borders the main traffic stream (flowing towards Mr MacDiarmid in his cottage on the outskirts). You will see that the poem manages to celebrate my usual Arcadian themes via somewhat unusual (and elliptical urban imagery – and that my own themes fit rather nicely into the general E. Conservation Year theme, of retaining the remote and pre-Socratic (as it were) basis of our civilisation – whose Incs and Ltds force it to consciously conserve itself. There is a further pleasing correspondence between the Incs (etc.) and the (traffic) island site – indeed, that's neater than a poet of nuances might hope for – as well as in the presence of the local shops (& Son). Indeed, all that is remarkably happy and to the point. Certainly, it is not exactly a Sundial inscription, but it does associate itself with the dial in a pleasing way.

As for the collaborative aspect, I don't know a great deal about Michael Harvey, but my catalogue of an Arts Council show, 'The Art of the Letter', assures me that he worked with Eric "Gill's one-time assistant, Joseph Cribb, at Ditchling", and has designed several type faces, including *Zephyr* and *Stamford Titling*. – He really is very well-known, and is jolly good (as well as helpful and enthusiastic).

Do you think, dear Stephen, that you could make anything by way of an explanatory essay, suitable for Biggar shops, out of this? Ah dearie me, I do set you some terrible tasks . . . I know that. But perhaps they have a wee element . . . of pleasure . . . in them . . . somewhere?

Needless to say, the Provost of Biggar will be forever in your debt . . . .

as will,
your old pal,

Ian

Canterbury
11 August 1970

Dear Ian,

In great haste – your letter arrived via Yorkshire yesterday & I have composed a piece of a few hundred words. I hope you don't find it too sentententious, if that is the word. It did seem to me that this particular exercise in public relations needed a bit of the obvious as well as a bit of the uncompromising.

Of course, you can alter anything that seems inaccurate or unnecessary (I put 'past few years' for residence in the vicinity of Biggar because the exact number eluded me).

After all that – many congratulations on the commission itself. It really is a splendid event, & Michael Harvey's cooperation must be a great step forward.

The Sunderland chap eventually wrote & his proposition seems entirely realistic. I imagine that the kind of essay I want to write is quite different from the one which would suit *Honey by the Water*. But it would be good if it could also find a public airing of a more accessible order.

I make my next swallow's swoop tomorrow – to Burgundy, Savoy & Alsace. With me goes a section of the complete [Francis] Ponge (who I hope to write on soon) & Thackeray's *Henry Esmond* (ditto). I should be back by 30 August.

Love to Sue, Eck & Ailie,
Yours

Stephen

Canterbury
2 September 1970

Dear Ian,

Here I am back in Canterbury, but with a minor affliction of the toe which at present serves as unwonted ballast to my prospective flights of fancy. Coupled with the appallingly hostile weather which succeeds the sultry ingratiating heat of France, this is making me unwilling to form very detailed plans for the future. I would like to come up to Stonypath some time next week – around 9/10 September. But there is this inhibiting factor – in any case, would that be a convenient time? I might be able to take in the supreme Germanic excess at the Edinburgh Festival on the way.[72]

I received & like so much 'Les Hirondelles', with its dedication. Did you get my piece about Biggar – & was it O.K.? I couldn't spend much time on it at that particular juncture. But I hope it passed muster, as I hope that the plan is prospering.

I have promised the Sunderland Gallery that I will produce something of about 5000 words by Oct. 1. A request for 500 words (separate and in addition) to go in the Northern Arts News, or something of the sort, arrived past its deadline (or rather, was waiting for me in an overdue state).

This is just a quick note, & more will follow. Love to Sue & Eck,

Yours Stephen

Stonypath
4 September [1970]

Dear Stephen,

I'm delighted to hear from you, as I have been wanting to thank you for your splendid response to my Wee Biggar request; I enclose the leaflet, and will send you further copies when – as I hope – the permanent edition with photograph has been printed. A couple of lines are not too well leaded, and I took the liberty of making a couple of small changes in your text – in

72. The principal art exhibition at the Edinburgh Festival of 1970 was of the German 'Blaue Reiter' group of Expressionist painters.

particular the bit about the Provost initiating the piece (as it was really him, and not the Council): I hope you wont mind my having done this – there was no way to have you approve the alterations*. [*It was not of course a Wild H. publication!]

The Sundial is now in place and is to be unveiled by "Lady T." this afternoon, with your leaflets being liberally distributed around. Michael Harvey spent a week here, cutting the letters, and all went well after the initial disasterous [sic] (as it seemed then) discovery, that the bit of slate which was supposed to arrive here when he did, was in fact still part of a Welsh hillside. Anyway, he made a very nice job, and I think the whole thing is very impressive indeed. A milestone, as it were – which at once suggests to me, that it would be a splendid idea to do a milestone of which you could write, that it represented a milestone in the poet's career.

Actually, this afternoon is to be rather milestony in general, as there is also the Press View of a Scottish Arts Council show of Wild Hawthorn things, in Glasgow; while in Edinburgh, The Scottish Arts C. is to confront Eric Walter White (But oh! His soul is black)[73] over the Fulcrum dispute.

Incidentally, you may tell as many people as possible, that the fiendish Rubinstein and Nash, have had to produce an explanation of their attitudes . . and there are signs that the Scottish Arts C. is not unaware that this is a somewhat unsatisfactory document.[74]

Into the lake
With the Eccles Cake

is the next move.

Talking of lakes, we have had 2 bulldozers in, and the new pond is someway towards completion. The weather (about which you so rightly complain) has, however, stopped work for the present, leaving us with a sea of mud where we are soon to have a sea. On such an area of water, a lot of nice things should be quite possible – regattas and goodness knows what.

73. Cf. William Blake, 'The Little Black Boy': 'And I am black, but O! my soul is white.'

74. The reference is to the still unfinished business of the 'Fulcrum Affair', Rubinstein and Nash being the solicitors acting on behalf of the Fulcrum Press. Viscount Eccles, Minister for the Arts, had at this stage been drawn into the dispute (see pp. 121, 126, 150).

I am very sorry to hear of your toe. If it can manage it, we would be most pleased to welcome you on the 9/10 dates you suggest. At the moment we are expecting Simon [Cutts] and Ian Gardner, but thereafter, very little is planned – a most unusual circumstance. It would be very nice to have you. – I only wish you could have seen Stonypath with Michael Harvey's hired caravan, and our 2 hired bulldozers, and the giant Atlas digging machine, and the Provost of Biggar's shooting-brake, and the County Surveyor's lorry awaiting the Sundial . . (which, by the way, weighs almost 4 cwts.).

I should have a few nice works to show you when you come – a nice new Finlay/Costley collaboration print, and perhaps one or two other things . . . As well as a semi-indoor sundial, with which you are also connected.

Sunderland is bobbing about at the back of my mind and will have to be gone into soon . . . .

Michael Harvey says he is very hopeful of our future collaborations, so that is a thought to cling to . . . .

We have a new sailingboat.

It is very nice to feel that you are back in this (or at least in that) country. And we will look forward to seeing you. Love,

Aye,

Ian

Canterbury
[pm 11 September 1970]

Dear Ian & Sue,

As you will realise, I can't manage to make the journey to Stonypath – as I am going into hospital to have a small operation on the offending toe. Many thanks for your royal blue letter & copy of the Biggar piece. I am delighted that it is now in situ. The longish essay which I promised is under way. Duncan Glen of *Akros* wrote to me about it – but I wonder if it is quite the thing for them?

Will write a real letter soon.

Yours Stephen

Stonypath
17 September 1970

Dear Stephen,

we do hope you are all right, and perhaps out of hospital by now? You do sound very sad and unlike your unusual (as it were) optimistic self. It there is any wee consolation we can offer, do not hesitate to let us know. We wish you (very) well.

We were most disappointed not to see you, and spent many hours looking hopefully down the long windblown spaces of our road, for your eager striding figure – not knowing you were toe-bound in England. I do hope your visit is only postponed, because – apart from all other considerations – you always cheer us up so much.

We seem to be having the (hostile) Indian Summer. It is as well to stay in one's wigwam.

I have a few things for you, but will hold on to them till I know if you will be coming, as they are rather awkward to post.

The Provost indicated his willingness to drive you over to see the famous Sundial, and I am sure this offer still stands. The Provost is a kind of negative of Montgomery, Eric. W. White, and the Lords Goodman and Eccles: he is one of those rare people who combine modesty with the ability to get things done. If nothing else, the Sundial has demonstrated that collaboration is entirely possible – a view I have often propounded.

I wonder if I told you that *The Scotsman* contrived to photograph, not the Sundial, but the water-hydrant on an adjacent traffic-island? It really would please me very much if you could write an article on the Sundial (when you have seen it, of course), for somewhere posh. I feel the Provost deserves this, for it took him only three weeks to manage what many supposed experts have claimed to be impossible for years ahead – the getting of a (post?) concrete poem in a public place.

Which reminds me, I had a most bizarre letter (which I am keeping to let you see) from Douglas Hall, of the Scottish National Gallery of Modern Art, performing inverse somersaults in offering me an exhibition in Stirling University. I have rarely seen such fury filtered through such a fine wee flute.

Which again reminds me, that we are all recovering from a monumental morning last Tuesday, when we had the long-awaited meeting between the film (you may remember there was supposed to be a film on my work) cameraman, an Arts Council official, a lady composer and myself. The film's Director was not of course present: he never is. Unluckily for himself, the cameraman (a thick-headed Glasgow-Italian git) divulged that the 2 wee films I was to be allowed to direct (as part of the total bargain, of bearing his fatuities), were to be cut from ten minutes each, to 3 minutes, as they were 'only little experimental films made by poets'. This was the last straw in what has been a barnyard of last straws, and it took me somewhat over 2 hours to express my feelings . . . at the end of which time, the cameraman resigned from all the films . . and departed for ever, in a flaming huff. I understand that he informed the Arts Council, in Edinburgh, that he is not only giving up the film, but is selling his house too --- a gesture which remains unexplained. It is one of those curious anomalies (spelling?), that all those present (except the lady composer and myself) had just taken a festival of obscene films, in their stride, and yet appeared to be horrified because I used what I believe the Arts C. official report is to call 'several oaths'. (Such as, to keep the record straight, 'You fucking thickheaded git' – an entirely objective comment which I'm prepared to justify in front of the £3000 worth of rushes they have taken so far.)

It is all very depressing. 'Little experimental films made by poets' indeed. Yughie Eyetie oaf.

.

Michael Harvey is proving an excellent collaborator, and we are ready to go ahead with 3 further projects for my garden. It is an **ENORMOUS** relief to have someone who <u>communicates</u>. A normal human being, in fact.

Now that September is here, do you think that the Great 'MD' mystery might be revealed, or should I say, unveiled, Stephen?

Now, we all send lots of love to you and hope we may hear from you soon. And perhaps we may see you before too awfully long?

Aye,

Ian

Canterbury
Sunday 20 Sept. [1970]

Dear Ian,

I am basking in a remarkably beautiful September day, though indoors at the moment away from the butterflies & the autumn crocuses which are displaying themselves in the garden. It is almost as if all the plants, having been through their regular cycle, are on the point of going into production again. I am even near to being convinced that the blackcurrant canes which I put in only ten days ago will produce a crop of new tender leaves from their budding shoots & so facilitate the creation of a final Glace à la Russe.[75]

It was equally fine yesterday. And I had arranged what turned out to be an idyllic meeting with Phil [Steadman] & Ruth [Brandon] at the intermediate point of Wye, where we lunched on plump partridges, bought antique lace for a shilling at an improbable exhibition, walked the carefully conserved downland above the Devil's Kneading Trough, & finally drank contemplatively under the trees by the River Stour. Phil had brought me back from USA a Jackson Pollock jigsaw puzzle – !

All this is a satisfactory form of convalescence for my tedious operation, which took place last Tuesday. I was given a general anaesthetic, hence totally insensible for a short period & liable to returning bouts of queasiness for a day or two. But it does seem as if the objective – to clear up infection and over-granulation on my toe – has been reached.

But of course this has ruled out any possibility of a visit to Stonypath. And it has prevented me from sending a 500 wd. piece on you to Sunderland for the Northern Arts News. But it hasn't stopped fairly steady progress on the much longer piece, which is fairly near completion. All that is wrong there is the irritating fact that I have mislaid (I am sure temporarily) the tiny 'Skylarks' poem which is an integral part of my argument. It must have found a nest within some large inviting envelope, or so I suspect.

I have made a tentative move towards *Art International* in relation to this article (supplementary to Sunderland publication). But Robert Kenedy is evidently thinking of some piece ultimately himself – & there is no need to anticipate that. I must make a reply to Douglas Glen, who wrote (on your

75. An ice flavoured with the leaves of blackcurrant bushes.

prompting, I think) enclosing the excellent Stephen Scobie article & suggesting a follow-up.[76] As I think I wrote before, *Akros* is not quite the place for what I am doing because of the lack of facilities for illustration if for no other reason. It would only tend to reinforce what seems to me (perhaps unjustly) to be the tendency of most of the *Akros* critics – to take criticism of a certain kind as applying exclusively to the 'visual arts' – & to treat that as tantamount to consignment to an outer darkness where no loyal Lallans-man[77] would dare to tread.

I wonder how the Biggar festivities, confrontations at the Scottish Arts Council etc. have passed? In all events, it will be splendid to hear news of your vastly aggrandised lochan/ocean & of all other events at Stonypath. It's a great shame this operation business has made me keep to Kent for all this time – & my movements are further complicated by the fact that I have already accepted (& incidentally spent) a Research Grant to go to Paris before term starts. However you see how it is . . .

To break the code of my earlier 'M.D.' references, have you yet seen (via Simon?) the catalogue of the July Maurice Denis exhibition? If not, tell me soon & if I get to Paris for a day or two, I will send you [one] on. It is jolly good.

All the best to Sue, Eck & Ailie –
Love

Stephen

Stonypath
23 September 1970

Dear Stephen,

how very nice it was to hear from you. This must be a fairly brief reply, as I seem to be involved in any number of controversies at the moment. However I do want to reply to you without delay.

76. Stephen Scobie, 'The Side-Road to Dunsyre', *Akros*, 15, August 1970.

77. The reference is to the term originally used by Robert Burns, but later applied to denote the literary language of the poets of the so-called 'Scottish Renaissance'. Finlay had always regarded this as an 'artificial language' (see *Midway*, p. 110).

First, we are most pleased to hear that you are recovering. However wee an operation may seem, it is a really quite serious thing, and shakes one's psyche. It is grand to know you are ok, and have been out and about. Your letter is such a Monet pastoral, that flowers would obviously be inappropriate and belated. Still, we all send lots and lots of good wishes . . . and the hope that your visit is only delayed?

I enclose Skylarks, which you had lost. And needed.

Now (I am answering all the bits in your letter), I am not at all sure that Mr Kenedy will really do a piece on my work for Art International. I hope he will; but unless by specific arrangement, you should not – I am sure – wait in his queue.

As regards Akros, I very much share your feelings about its general ethos. On the other hand, I hate to scorn an olive branch, and a surprising number of people seem to have seen (and enjoyed) S. Scobie's piece in the last one.[78] I realise that there is a strict limit to the number of essays you can write on me. All the same, I hope you may reconsider the Akros possibility – the more so as I had a rather pleasant note from Mr Glen today, saying that he will gladly have blocks made, if I send a selection of our new poem/prints for him to reproduce. I suppose it would be impractical to use the same piece in Sunderland, Akros . . . and Zurich? The thing is, if you don't write for Akros, who on earth will? I mean, that is a question to shudder over, on winter nights.

As regards 'MD', no, I have not seen the Denis catalogue, and now that the opportunity is in the offing, I will scarcely be able to sleep for excitement. Whew. Maurice Denis . . . The very name is like a bell . . . Off to Paris with you at once. On wings, on wings.

I enclose a cutting for your pleasure. The MAN ON THE RIGHT is Maurice Lindsay, 'self-styled' leading Scottish poet, and head of The Civic Trust. The umbrella was to defend himself against Mrs H. Macd. (Hugh the First, as the Provost always calls him).[79]

78. See note 74. The article discussed both Finlay and Hugh MacDiarmid, with insight and tact.

79. The press cutting, from the *Hamilton Advertiser* of 11 September 1970, showed an official grouping around the newly installed Biggar sundial. Maurice Lindsay, with his umbrella, is standing on the right, holding a finger to his nose, 'simply baffled' as the caption reads. The brief article concludes: 'The sun dial has an inscription by well-known poet Ian Finlay from Hamilton'.

I am building a model of The Queen Mary (the ship).

Tomorrow, Sue, Eck, and Ailie depart for London, where Eck is to carry the train (Toot toot chuff chuff) at Sue's brother's wedding – to a very posh Deb, (who has a charming air, nonetheless, of holding her stockings up with elasticbands, and of being about to turn into a warm suet-pudding). Eck and Ailie have produced gigantic colds for the ocassion. (Or however you spell that: I expect Simon would know).

By the way, have you looked me up in Debrett?

There seems to be a lot of news I ought to give you, but in spite of everything I retain the feeling that we will see you soon. So I will pass over a lot of wee items. It has been a rather curious time.

[. . .]

Well, dear old Stephen Twinkletoes, I look forward to hearing from you. I am so glad you are ok. Have a nice time in Paris. Love from us all,

Aye,

Ian

PS A very strange sequel to Skylarks is being printed at present. It resembles nothing so much as a collaboration between Larionov and Gertrude Stein.

Stonypath
30 September [1970]

Dear Stephen,

I have been very concerned about not having written you, after getting your essay.[80] Sue (as I mentioned) has been in London, and in the meanwhile we have had Stuart staying: the large dog and small child, made correspondence impossible. I am awfully sorry.

80. 'Ian Hamilton Finlay: Engineer and Bricoleur', booklet (7pp) included as part of *Ceolfrith* 5 (folder of work by Finlay published by Ceolfrith Bookshop Gallery, Sunderland, 1970). The antithesis implied in the title, and developed throughout the essay, comes from Claude Lévi-Strauss's *La Pensée sauvage* (1962: English translation, *The Savage Mind* , 1966).

Our letters have been crossing so much recently, and it is perhaps already too late to make my comments on the essay.

Well, of course, it is too late, as I see you are in Paris. So, I think --- for 'future use' or however one should put it – we might discuss the essay when you come up. Broadly speaking, I feel a wee bit worried about The Savage Mind, since I feel that you tend, a wee bit, to attribute to Levi-Strauss (whose waltzes have always delighted me), some of the things which are traditionally of the essence of art. The problem here is, that we live in a decade which has entirely repudiated art as we knew it – while the method of art (which is certainly a particular method) is so ingrained in me, that I find it almost impossible to set it out as a series of propositions. In short, I'm non-plussed. It's not that I feel your essay is entirely on the wrong lines, but that I feel that Oscar Wilde is a better reference-point than Levi-Strauss – or that what I am doing is more understandable in the terms of 18th century aesthetics, than in those of 20th century anthropology.

There are also some particulars which I would like to discuss with you.

Meanwhile, I will by no means feel it a disaster if your essay is printed in Sunderland in its present form.

Nor, dear Stephen, are you to think me ungrateful: for you are one of the few people who I really count on – whose merely being there, somewhere, is a gratification, and a reassurance.

.

I will make this a short letter, as I am feeling a bit depressed over my Fulcrum troubles. On Saturday, I am to receive my copies of a rather pretty, new, wee Wild Hawthorn publication – in almost as many colours as Jacob's coat.[81] So you will be having one shortly. The larger items can wait for your visit, as – like me – they can be crushed. I hope you are safely back from Paris . . . and was glad that your letter demonstrated that your toe had not gone to your head. Love,

Aye,

Ian

81. *Fishing News, News*, with drawings by Margot Sandeman, was hand-printed at the Salamander Press. Taking the form of a concertina, and involving a range of printing inks, it was indeed a virtuoso performance by the printer Michael Glen.

Canterbury
8 Oct. 70

P.S. M.D. enclosed![82]

Dear Ian,

Thank you so much for your letter, and especially for the many-coloured *Fishing News* News, which is a great and unexpected delight (in the sense that one never knew you had so much more up your sleeve . .). I am enclosing the more refined version of the Sunderland article, which may make a few things clearer, but which is unlikely to resolve your very understandable doubts.

I think you put your finger on the dilemma when you mention our 'decade which has entirely repudiated art'. What I have tried to do in the essay (and what I have been edging towards for some time) is precisely a method of recovering a general theory of human creativity according to which art might once again acquire an absolute value. I am entirely in sympathy with you when you say that your work is much more readily accessible through Oscar Wilde than through *La Pensée Sauvage*. And yet, surely the tragic thing about Classical culture is that it assumes as a pre-condition a collection of people knowing something in common. One cannot somehow re-invent, or re-interpret for our times (!), in my view, the entirety of Classical culture – and yet it is precisely in that entirety, and in the common consciousness of those participating in it, that the secret of communication in art resides.

So one is obliged, it seems to me, to try and make use of a kind of anthropological entirety – to proceed from the impossibility of assuming a common cultural code to the possibility of divining a common cultural armature, or structure, within humanity as a whole. This is the method of Rousseau (and no one could claim it to be more than second best) – it is also the implication of Lévi-Strauss, and his followers.

I am sure you will recognise the difficulty of the position, and perhaps you would accept that such a discussion of your work in outlandish terms might not be so glaring in France, where there is an innate disposition to Classicism, and an equal readiness to see the insights of Structuralism in Classicist terms. I am now eager to translate my essay into French, I may say, consequent upon

82. The long awaited Maurice Denis catalogue.

the distinct possibility being offered by the French magazine *L'Oeil*. (This fits in with my recent conclusion that the state of cultural division between England and Europe has now become so grave that I am obliged to write a certain kind of article in French and publish it in a French magazine because otherwise it would be literally incomprehensible:[83] the point is that one has no overall context, simply a number of distinct sub-contexts, for critical discourse).

But I must add that Black Sparrow have asked me for a short introduction to *Honey by the Water*, and I am not likely to see that assignment in such terms. It is more a question of hinting, as the Sparrow man suggested, why the robe of Concrete poetry is very far from being seamless.

I must get back to the hurly-burly of the term. Could you send the article back fairly soon, as I could then post it to *L'Oeil*, if you thought that a good plan. All best wishes to Sue, Ailie and train-bearer Eck (I bore a train at his age, but so exhausted myself learning the first verse of 'Praise my soul, the king of heaven' that I had no room for smoked salmon . . .)

Yours

Stephen

Canterbury
22 October [19]70

Dear Ian,

Very many thanks for the welcome letter, also to Sue for her charming card. The 'Mozart' and 'Zulu' prints are really lovely[84] – I am charmed by the coal-black quality of the latter. And the 'Beehives' card is splendid.[85] I did appreciate the bibliography, and I know that Seamus Cooney

83. My article, 'L'anti-histoire de Henry Esmond', on Thackeray's novel, had been offered to English and American academic journals, before being accepted for publication (in translation) by the editors of the new French literary periodical, *Poétique*, launched in 1970 under the auspices of Roland Barthes. Its appearance in English had to wait until the appearance of my book, *The Clothing of Clio*, in 1984.

84. *Homage to Mozart*, with Ron Costley, screen print, and *Scottish Zulu*, with David Button, screen print.

85. *A Use for Old Beehives*, with Richard Demarco, folding card.

of Black Sparrow would like one too (he mentioned it in a recent letter).

I am entering a period of insane social whirling, finding myself embarked from tonight on a series of three dinners/parties with students (the third involving me in a cherry-coloured velvet doublet, slashed hose and a feather bonnet) followed by three dinners in London (the second of which, with the notorious Philippe Sollers and Julia Kristeva of Tel Quel,[86] I am on the point of abandoning through sheer terror), and finally capped by three elaborate affairs here in Canterbury. And indeed this particular round comes after a number of memorable occasions in the near past, including a dinner with the great Cardinal-Archbishop of Malines-Brussels (Suenens) who gave everyone here a kind of spiritual refreshment usually neither expected nor found in ecclesiastical discourse. It seemed quite natural to be chatting after dinner to someone who had known, and was speaking about, Pope John.

Away from these reflections – I must first of all reply to your query about the French magazine. Since you have a recent set of superb photos, and since they would probably decide whether to go ahead with the article chiefly on the basis of the photos, it might be a good idea to send a batch fairly soon to:

Mme Monique Schneider-Maunoury
L'Oeil
3 Rue Séguier
Paris 6

I could send a quick note explaining that these were what they were. What do you think?

After a lot of indecision, I sent Duncan Glen the Sunderland article, explaining the position about it. He had said that he felt only he could judge whether it would fit in with the other contents, and I suppose he is right there. As you might have guessed from the ref. to Seamus Cooney (should people in Los Angeles really have names like that?), the preface for Honey by the Water is arranged, for some time before the end of the year. He says he is more and more delighted by the whole project the further it goes.

What I must address my mind to is a date for a weekend visit to Stonypath. It should be quite easy once these present waves have subsided (as one might

86. This was one of the first of the many occasions on which the hospitable Director of the French Institute, André Zavriew, invited me to meet the luminaries of the current French intellectual scene.

say). It will be so nice to see you all again. But I wonder if summer has now finally fled from the moors of Lanark? Here it returns miraculously as if unwilling to let us go, and the gardens are all thoroughly confused by the outrageous recidivism: my marigolds think it is Spring, and my roses are totally rejuvenated.

Love to all of you,

Stephen

Stonypath
27 October [1970]

Dear Stephen,

I suppose it is very tedious that my letters almost always begin by saying how nice it was to hear from you. But then, that's the fact.

Velvet doublet, slashed hose . . . and why are you dressing up as Bonnie Prince Charlie?

And who on earth is "the notorious Philippe Sollers . ." He sounds foreign to me. I once knew a man called Philippe and he was French. Beware.

I hope that Cardinal-Archbishop has nothing to do with those Low Country liberalising tendencies one has read of? Perhaps he is a Worker Cardinal-Archbishop.

Ah, Seamus Cooney. Stephen, I must warn you that Mr Cooney is really unbearable: Sue wakes up in the middle of the night, muttering **COONEY COONEY** . . . and even Stuart Mills blanches when you mention his name. He is long known to us as the arch, indeed the worker arch, complainer and fusser about/over Wild Hawthorn parcels. Quite intolerably superior – and always given to supposing that he has missed some item, which he turns out to have, after all – but not till you have sent it off.. When I had signed my contract with Black Sparrow, it at once behaved like a Q-ship, throwing aside its innocent hatches and revealing – who ? Why, Seamus Cooney. – Mr Cooney will be supervising your book. Good luck. (And you will need it too . . . .)

As a matter of fact, I have just been forced to write to Black Sparrow confessing that I cannot manage Mr Cooney any longer. He is beyond me. I conceded him the need for a few factual notes, of the briefest sort, to accompany the poems. By the time I had his most recent letter, he was – in entire seriousness – demanding a footnote explaining the word "flake" in the 'Russian' poem about battleships in the snow[87] ------ not to speak of a footnote to explain the word "tanker" in "fleet tankers": "not oil tankers, surely?".

This went too far and I demurred. Indeed some might say I demurrrrrrred. Enough, I said, can bear it no longer. I have contracted to send one book, and a book on that book is another book. You must explain this to Mr Cooney.

You see, Stephen, the wretched Cooney collects my letters, and Simon even went so far as to sell him some . . . . So that he stops at nothing to wring another paragraph from me . . . and (as I said to the Black Sparrow itself) I will, if we go on at this rate, be flat on my back with my head in a whirl, before we ever start upon the book.

Mr Cooney also took it upon himself to re-type my ms (which is no doubt destined for his private collection). I have suggested that the proper place for my ms at this minute, would be the printer's . . . . It is all very perplexing.

·

Stephen, when you refer to "a recent superb set of photos" which do you mean? Do you mean the ones I sent to Mr Kenedy? The photos I can get, are all photos destined for the German book, and there seems no reason why the German publisher should not be pleased to have some of them in the French magazine, esp. if the magazine could make reference to the fact that a book will be forthcoming. On the other hand, I can order copies specially from the photographer, purchasing them myself, and this what I did for Mr Karpel. The bill came to £14, which is possible, but not something I want to do lightly. If, though, I told the photographer that the magazine would perhaps use the photos and pay her, then she would surely be willing to do them on that basis. Please tell me a) what you think is a sensible scheme; and b) what sort of photos you'd like – a selection of poems and activities (boats, water, kites?)

87. *After the Russian*, originally published with John Furnival (Openings Press, 1969) was to appear in Black Sparrow Press's *Honey by The Water*. The 'tanker' query would have been provoked by the sundial design, 'The Four Seasons as Fleet Tankers', also to be included in this selection.

The box has at last gone off to Mr Karpel, and this I will deal with in my next letter to you.

I am delighted that your Stonypath weekend is coming nearer.

And that you liked the Zulu . . Ah, the gleaming ebony of their skins.

Do not (social) whirl away altogether. Love,

Ian

Canterbury
8 November 1970

Dear Ian,

A very quick letter to thank you for yours & for 'Private Tutor' (with memories of the Hunts. Ouse)[88] & to suggest that I might come up to Stonypath this coming weekend – Saturday 14 November – for a couple of days. Is that at all possible? I fear the onset of winter winds & all manner of natural impediments in addition to that man-made, but hazardous period, the exam season, if I don't take the chance to visit you fairly soon.

Could I, incidentally, still manage to get a bus from the Bus Station if I arrived in Edinburgh at 6.30pm? I am hoping so.

Sorry to hear of the concealed depths of Seamus Cooney – he sounds as if he is almost literally preying on you. Do let us hope the book is not adversely affected by his attitude –

Proofs from Sunderland were promised but haven't arrived yet. I spoke to C. Carrell on the phone & heard that they have been asked to do a greater yet exhibition of your work (is that it?). I suppose I might even just possibly be able to squeeze in a visit to this one if I pass through Newcastle on my way up or down.

It is a great pleasure to envisage seeing all of you again. I suppose Ailie will

88. Issue 12 of PRIVATE TUTOR (a fly-sheet published by the Tarasque Press) was devised by Finlay, and included a one-letter poem under the title St. Ives (Hunts.) Boat. The letter was 'S'.

now be about where Eck was when I last saw him (in terms of advancement so to speak). I look forward to hearing from you.

love

Stephen

The visit that had been deferred because of the operation on my toe took place as planned over the course of this mid-November weekend. As a result of several discussions around the fire-side, I returned from Stonypath with a sheet of paper on which Finlay had inscribed an immediate agenda for me:

Read

Pater's Imaginary Portraits
Goncourt Brothers French Painting

Write books on
The Glasgow Boys

Obtain
Poussin & the Elegaic [sic] Tradition,
From Meaning In the Visual Arts

Action
Retrieve submarine from Mr Kenedy

[My own note] Article to **KARPEL** (parcel sent end of Oct.)

Most of these commissions were executed in the following months, though I was unable to come to terms with the modern Scottish painters known as 'The Glasgow Boys' until I had the opportunity to visit their outstanding retrospective exhibition at Kelvingrove Art Gallery, Glasgow, in 2010. Our discussions at Stonypath had turned in the direction of Panofsky's celebrated essay, 'Et in Arcadia Ego: Poussin and the Elegiac Tradition'. As indicated in the letters that follow, I received a second prompting to forward Finlay a copy of this text, which would take on considerable importance in planning future developments in the garden. The copied text was despatched to Stonypath in early December.

In addition to these obligations, high priority was given on my return to exchanging a pair of mittens I had brought as a present for the Finlays' young daughter Ailie, which were not a good fit.

Oxford
Wednesday [pm 25 November 1970]

Dear Ian & Sue,

It is so remiss of me not to write before and thank you for the splendid, sparkling stay, which sustained me through a re-entry into the misty gloom of autumnal England. I'll write very soon, and send Ailie's **MITTENS**. But for the moment I am still on the move & pausing only a minute or two among dreaming spires. The Sunderland catalogues were announced as being on their way & will, I hope, arrive in time for Bernard Lassus[89] (& the photographs, I also hope). I'll send a catalogue to Karpel immediately, as arranged.

Love to all of you

Stephen

Stonypath
1 December [1970]

Dear Stephen,

I hope the photos arrived in time.

89. The French landscape designer Bernard Lassus, whose work I had followed since the mid-1960s, had begun to express a strong interest in Finlay's work at Stonypath. He later wrote a preface for the compilation featuring David Paterson's photographs of the garden (*Selected Ponds, West Coast Poetry Review*, 1975). He visited Finlay at Stonypath for the first time in July 1976.

Will it be possible to send the

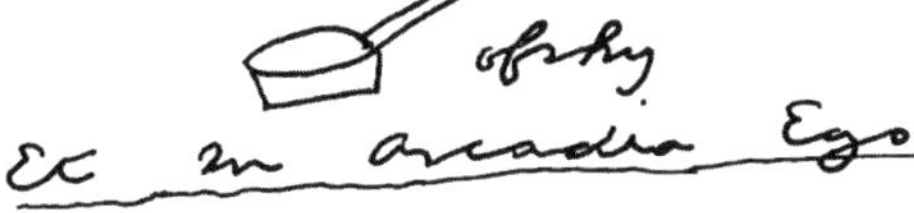

unravelling, soon, as I am most eager to see it.

Further favour: Dear Stephen, could you send me, By Return of Post, a brief synopsis (each) of 6 Classical love-stories, such as, i.e. Daphnis & Chloe (which I already know) . . . You need not stick to Greece. A few sentences on each will suffice.

Love,

Ian

PS From anyone else, the above request would be enigmatic: but in my case you will realise that it is connected with fishing boats . . . .

Canterbury
Thursday [3 December 1970]

Dear Ian,

Here, by return, are six classical and one bonus love story, composed by myself and a friend in the dark watches of the night, & a testimony to the common cultural heritage of our nation.[90]

Will write at the weekend. The photos did indeed arrive in time.

Love to all,

Stephen

90. My recollection of the particular classical love-stories that were chosen on this occasion is hazy, but the selection certainly included Hero and Leander. There seems to be no project from this period that corresponds directly to Finlay's intimation of a new work associating such stories with 'fishing boats'. But a later work for the Bruglingen Gardens, Basel (undertaken in collaboration with Nicholas Sloan in 1984) involves five oval tree-plaques inscribed with the names of classical lovers.

Canterbury
Sunday 6 Dec. [1970]

Dear Ian,

Finally I have a few minutes of unearthly calm, at that Sunday-morning juncture when the only sound to be heard is the lethargic clinking of milk-bottles. We have, that is to say, got over the lengthy tribulations of the **PART ONE** examination & the field is left for more or less celebratory activities heralding the approach of Xmas. To me, this particular week will always be distinguished, I feel, by an excessive – if not completely repugnant – indulgence in **PHEASANTS**: I calculate that out of my 6 next dinners, at least 4 are guaranteed to be of pheasant (two on home ground, two at official dinners partly arranged by myself), the remainder being in one case of hare & in the other of nothing predictable.

Which brings me inevitably to remembering that splendid weekend at Stonypath, & its delightful, wholly freakish weather. I have now actually got (i.e. changed) Ailie's mittens, & will send them in the course of the week, when I have a substantial envelope.

I hope you got the classical love-stories & found them à propos. They caused a great deal of amusement in the composition. I decided that, rather than fish around in dictionaries of mythology, I should spin them out directly in consultation (with the student friend, incidentally, for whom I took a *Fishing News News*) & thus exploit something amounting to a common cultural memory (based on the solid rock of the classical education). But this means, I suppose, that there may be significant lapses, omissions & indeed, possibly, errors.

Thank you so much for the little 'Heart shape', which is really splendid.[91] I shall have it framed, in a minute frame, & possibly hang it side by side with my largest/smallest painting – a sympathetic re-exploration of Delacroix's *Femmes d'Algers* reduced from absurdly large proportions to the fey perfection of a colour photograph.

The photos arrived in time & I was able to show them to Bernard Lassus. This was a very good thing, because he warned me (as I might have realised) that I should make very sure to explain them to the rédactrice of *L'Oeil* ( ), as

91. *A Heart-Shape*, with Ron Costley.

they are puzzling, particularly so, to someone with little or no English. He also suggests that I should select about ½ to ¾ of the ensemble, & make a connected exposé of them. I think he is right, considering the language difficulty and the magazine itself.

What has not arrived, parbleu, is the bundle of catalogues from Ceolfrith (no doubt erratically proceeding by coracle from Holy Island). The card announcing their departure came at least a fortnight ago. But, significantly, the proofs of the article were similarly announced as having been sent off & only reached me ten days later. No wonder Lord Hall got the push . . .[92]

It has now become as black as night, though midday, & I am expected for drinks on the other side of Canterbury. I'll write again at a shorter interval than last time. I shall be in Yorkshire from about 19 Dec. & taking a week in Holland in early January.

Love to Sue, Eck & Ailie
Yours

Stephen

Stonypath
12 December 1970

Dear Stephen,

thank you so much for the beautiful series of Historical Love Affairs. They are quite worth publishing as they are. I am delighted to have them --- and to have a friend who makes such a noble response. Please thank The Student, too. If the outcome eventuates from the circumstance – as Simon would say – with the entire conviction that he was writing Mallarméan prose – I shall let you both see it -----

and that 'it', like a basket without a balloon, is a fine Cuttsian touch.

92. The postcard sent by Christopher Carrell to announce that my catalogues had been posted arrived shortly after my return from Stonypath in mid-November. The ensuing delay in the arrival of the package was no doubt a symptom of the worsening labour disputes in the postal service. Lord Hall had recently resigned from the post of Chairman of the United Kingdom General Post Office.

Thank you also for Panofsky. This is a super essay. It is missing pages 350, & 351, and if these could ever be added – with their mossy steps in the argument – I would be very pleased. You probably have no idea how much pleasure I got from reading this essay. It was a huge pleasure for me. I am keeping it to hand.

I do hope the Christmas Carrell sent you the catalogues by now. When he rang, I asked him if they had been sent, and though he said 'Yes', (this was a good wee while ago, now) there was a certain lack of conviction in his voice.

And I am glad the photos did get to you, and I hope that magazine --- spelling it is not only beyond me but against my chauvinistic principles – will be able to use them, together with your commentary.

I have decided it is high time I am famous and rich. Instead of famous and poor and unknown.

Very sillily, or sililly, I sent your Christmas card to Almondbury . . where I hope it will await you. Your C. present is still at the printer! If it is dripped on by candles – as I hear things are, nowadays – it will only add to its effect. And farther than that from Mondrianism, Finlay cannot go . . . . . .

I got the Stedelijk concrete catalogue.[93] Oh dear. Apart from my own personal feelings, at being lumped in with Sharkey etc., (the Wild Hawthorn's role has been carefully reduced to Nil, by Mr Cobbing), it must be said that the whole thing is a horrid mush, of almost spectacular lack of talent, bad typesetting, and terrible taste. It is like the Decade After The Decade Before. It is also – somehow – infuriating to see Mr Dom Sylvester described (self-described?) as the leading critic of everything . . and my own constructions lumped in with those who still use letraset and string. Obviously the Manifesto is all. Stereodeadphones has eclipsed the Wild Hawthorn Press.

The Stedelijk also sent a photo of my Sails poem, standing on its veranda, or whatever you call it, ('steading' is the word that comes to me but it is not that . . . .)

Instead of getting in the Girl Guides, as I had suggested, the wretched Stedelijkians have tethered the poem's rear-leg to a bit of iron . . . and if that

93. The catalogue of the exhibition, *Sound texts?/Concrete Poetry/Visual texts*, which took place at the Stedelijk Museum, Amsterdam, in 1970, and included work by Finlay.

is not enough, they have ignored my careful diagram, and advice as to sailor's knots . . and got all the rigging looking the way that Eck gets his shoelaces . . And the Dutch were, you know, a Seafaring Nation . . . .

My Faith is shattered.

Eric Walter White has entered The Christmas Competition.

Meanwhile, I have installed a splendid new Sundial – a work of pristine classic purity, a shiver of romance in limpid armour, a warm icicle, a sliver of infinity . . . .[94]

I have a splendid new poem to send you, but will keep it for January, as a consolation.

If you see anything else like that delightful Panofsky, let me know . . .

Love and gratitude, Aye,

Ian

any news of your Introduction?

Clough House
Almondbury
Huddersfield
30 December [19]70

Dear Ian,

I must thank you first of all for your letter of early December, secondly for the delightful twin-counterpart Xmas card that was waiting for

94. This is probably the 'Evening will come' sundial, carved by John Thorpe, which was installed beside the Middle Pond and photographed by me the following year. > pl. 7

me at home, & thirdly for the really splendid 'Fuseli' which arrived shortly afterwards.[95] It is a great triumph, not least in the technical domain (because I have really no idea how it has come to have such a finish and quality). I have pressed it into service in a slight way in the enclosed Foreword (of which more later).

I was glad the Love Affairs survived their midnight compilation & were acceptable. Also that Panofsky was a success. Alas, I have no access at present to mossy steps 350–351, but will seek them out on my return to Kent.

We have been enjoying (?) here what is somewhat unconvincingly reported as better weather than in the South. I have adapted myself to a fairly strict regime of ingestion and production on the literary level. In go, principally, Webster, Henry James & Sidney Keyes. Your gift of the Guenther biographical enquiry has led to a chain of events relating to Keyes, of which the most recent is the indication by one of my students that his father knew K. well in the last months in Tunisia (he has gone away with a vacation assignment to fulfil on the topic).[96] I managed to find the 1945 collected poems in a London bookshop & have been slowly perusing them.[97]

Webster is a deep, dark mine that I have never previously essayed. I am between readings of the *Duchess of Malfi.*

Henry James is really the most central to me at the moment – really *late* (?well-hung) Henry James: in other words, *The Wings of the Dove*. I find that James reveals, in a curiously direct way, breathtakingly vast reserves of sensitivity, nuance & implication in human behaviour, & above all that, unlike, say, Proust, he really transmits a belief in the possibility (& necessity) of human communication (for good or ill) at a variety of interweaving levels. He makes me feel how thoroughly <u>nice</u> and <u>exciting</u> it is (or could be) to be a human being.

95. 'Xmas Rose', the Finlays' card for 1970 and poem/print no. 14, was the twin of 'Xmas Star', their card for 1969, which had also been drawn by John Furnival. *Archangel* ('A Full-Rigged Ship/ In the manner of Fuseli') was a lithograph, which used the calligraphy of Sidney McK. Glen to evoke the misty atmosphere of the paintings of the Swiss artist, Henry Fuseli (1741–1825).

96. Finlay had lent me a copy of John Guenther, *Sidney Keyes – A biographical enquiry*, published by London Magazine editions in 1967. The poet Keyes had died on armed service in Tunisia in 1943.

97. *The Collected Poems of Sidney Keyes*, London: Routledge, 1945.

From the productive side of things, I have so far written a fairly large piece on Bernard Lassus, all about English gardens and French roofless rooms in the Edward Hyams idiom. It should be appearing, after a little more thought has been expended on it, in *Art & Artists*.[98]

Secondly, there is the Foreword which you see enclosed. I shall be eager to hear what you think of it. (I shall be anxious to settle the question of whether a sea-poppy has stamens &, if not, what does it have?) The problem seemed to me to be one of combining a general introduction to the span of your work with a lead-in to the poems. I think that I have solved it fairly successfully, but am just a little hesitant when I think of Los Angeles. Do Americans know what sine qua non's are? (let alone metonyms –).

If you were able to reply very quickly, I could send off the top copy to Black Sparrow immediately. It would have to be before Monday, as then I am off to Holland for a day or two. And I would like, if possible, to send it before long, as I promised it for the end of 1970.[99] Most important, could you send their address if you do reply? I have left their letters at Canterbury.

Infuriatingly enough, the Carrell copies had not arrived there when I left. I shall have to send him a line pointing this out. It means that I have not yet been able to write to B. Karpel.

I must catch the post now, wishing you all the very best of New Years –

Yours

Stephen

98. 'Bernard Lassus: Ambiance', *Art and Artists*, June 1971, pp. 20–23. As already noted, the French landscape artist Bernard Lassus had begun to develop an interest in Finlay's work at Stonypath.

99. Despite my expressions of haste, the publishing schedule of Finlay's *Honey by the Water* soon lapsed. The collection eventually appeared in 1973, by which time my 'Foreword' had been recast as an 'Afterword'.

PLATES

1. Ian Hamilton Finlay sailing on Lochan Eck, with Stephen Bann on shore.
Photograph by Anthony Grist (5 September 1971).

2 (top). The Biggar Sundial, installed September 1970.
Photograph by Diane Tammes (1970).

3 (above). The Canterbury Sundial, installed December 1972.
Photograph by James Styles (1973).

4 (top). Rose-lore garden bench, stone, with Vincent Butler, 1970.
Photograph by Diane Tammes (c. 1970).

5 (above). Tree bench, oak, with Vincent Butler, 1971.
Photograph by George Oliver (1971).

6. House Pond (later Temple Pond), with Carved Stone and dovecote.
Photograph by Anthony Grist (5 September 1971).

7. Sundial ('Evening will come'), wood with gnomon, beside the Middle Pond (under construction), with John Thorpe, 1970.
Photograph by Stephen Bann (September 1971).

8. Four Seasons Sundial (third in series), oak, with John Thorpe, 1970.
Photograph by Anthony Grist (5 September 1971).

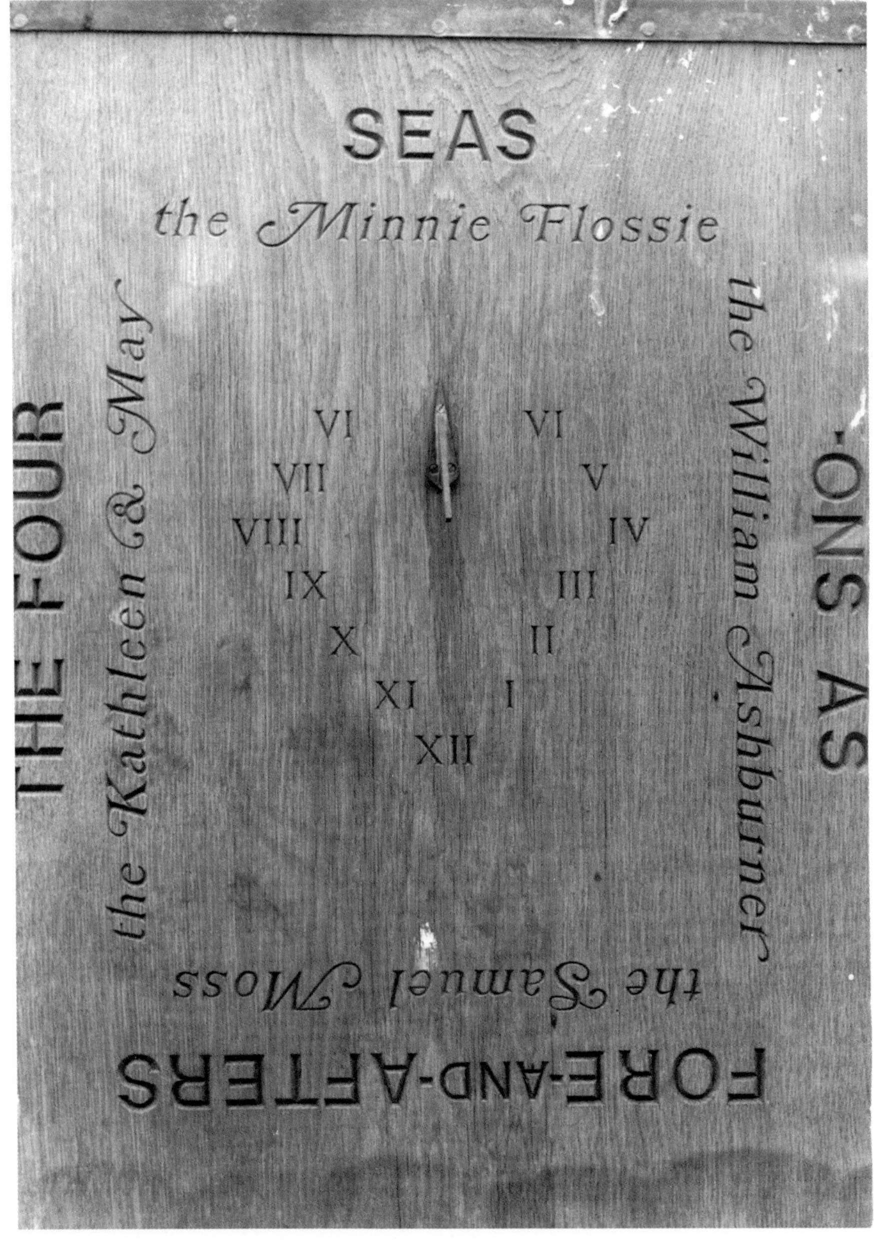

9. Four Seasons Sundial (third in series), oak, with John Thorpe, 1970.
Photograph by Diane Tammes (c. 1970).

10 (top). Sundial (Fragments/Fragrance), stone, with Maxwell Allan, 1970. *Photograph by Anthony Grist (5 September 1971).*

11 (above). Ian Hamilton Finlay and Stephen Bann on the new wooden bridge to the Top Pond. *Photograph by Anthony Grist (5 September 1971).*

12. Silver Cloud, table tomb, inscribed marble, with Michael Harvey, 1972.
Photograph by James Styles (1973).

13 (above). Curfew/Curlew, wild stone, with Vincent Butler, 1971. *Photograph by Anthony Grist (5 September 1971).*

14 (opposite, top). Ian Hamilton Finlay and Stephen Bann, in front of the sundial (Tristram's Sail) in the House Pond. *Photograph by Anthony Grist (10 July 1972).*

15 (opposite, below). Sundial (Tristram's Sail), circle of slate on rusticated stone base, with Michael Harvey, 1971. *Photograph by James Styles (1973).*

TRISTRAM'S SAIL · SHADOW · WIND ·
The shadow
has an axis which is
the apparent wind direction.
Outwardly from the boat it cannot
extend for an infinite distance and its
area becomes narrower the further away
from the boat one moves. The effect is said
to be felt up to seven mast lengths away.

16. Planting by the House Pond: Ian Hamilton Finlay and Sue Finlay.
Photograph by Anthony Grist (10 July 1972).

17. Planting by the House Pond: Ian Hamilton Finlay, Sue Finlay and Stephen Bann. *Photograph by Anthony Grist (10 July 1972).*

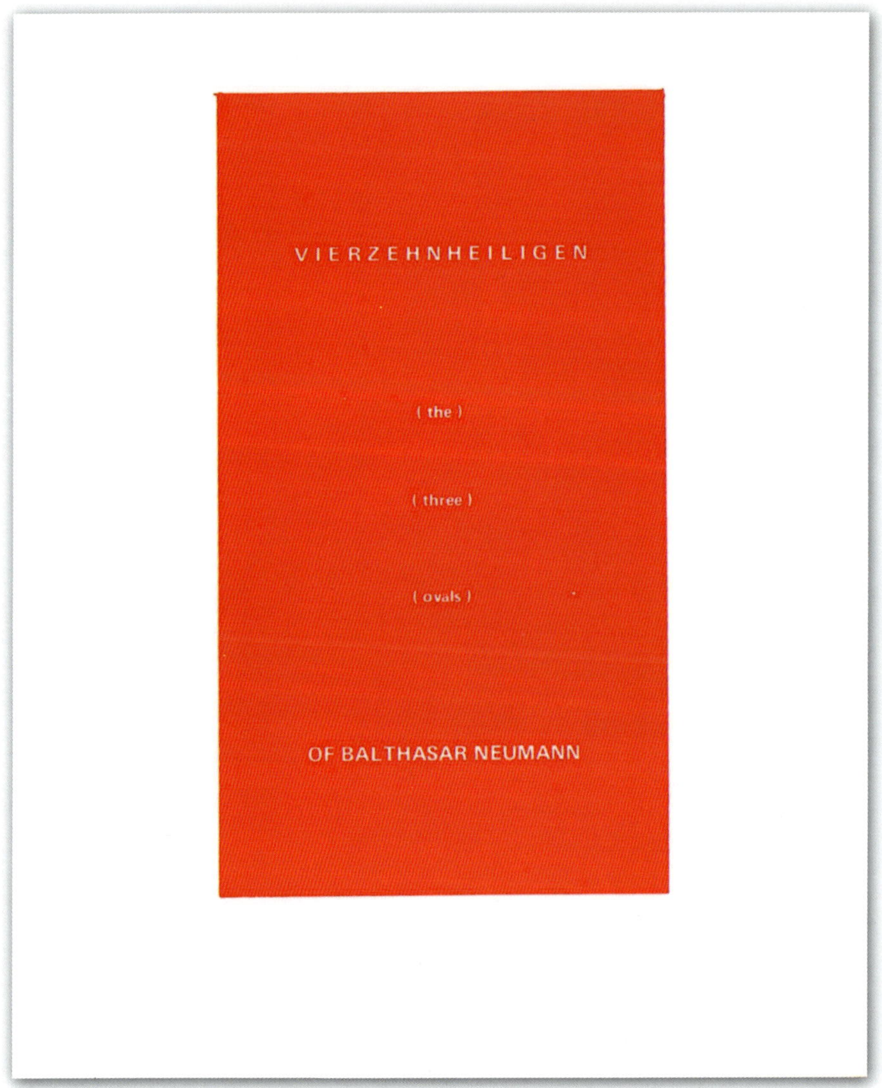

18. Stephen Bann, *Vierzehnheiligen*, poem-card, Tarasque Press, 1970.

19. Stephen Bann, The Garden as a Parenthesis, silk-screen print by Bob Chaplin (1980), after poem-card, Tarasque Press, 1971.

20. Feeding the fish: Ian Hamilton Finlay and his family.
Photograph by Anthony Grist (10 July 1972).

II

January 1971–January 1972

My New Year had begun with a brief trip to Holland, in the course of which I visited the Dutch constructive artist, Joost Baljeu, who was contributing to my anthology, The Tradition of Constructivism. *In my foregoing letter of 30 December 1971, I had referred to Finlay's gift of a biographical memoir of the English poet, Sidney Keyes. I also mentioned that I had managed to find a copy of the 1945 edition of Keyes's collected poems. This prompted Finlay to launch into his vivid autobiographical reminiscences of visits to England during the period of the Second World War.*

Stonypath
9 January 1971

Dear Stephen,

I hope you are safely back from The Land of the Windmills. This is a brief and belated reply to your nice letter of 30 December 1970. If I say 'belated' it is because, in retrospect, The Festive Season has come to seem like one of those awful sea passages throughout which one is hurled about endlessly, till one loses all sense of Time. How pleasant it is to waken and to discover that it is neither January 1st nor December 25th.

The kids had flu for a <u>very</u> long time, and I had exhaustion, and Sue had a cut finger, and then everyone had New Year very badly, for days and days, during which there was no post or paper. After that it froze so hard that the Postie could not get up and – like some terrible echo of Christmas – we got our letters about 4.30 every day, in time to read them in the gathering Dark.

I would love to read your essay on French roofless rooms and English gardens.[1] How prolific you are, Stephen, how talented, how 18th century . . . (How sensible, how nice).

As for S. Keyes, I am glad you liked the little book on him. Since you are interested in his background, I will surprise you by my own reminisces of SK (note the initials):

1. This was my essay, 'Bernard Lassus: Ambiance', to be published in *Art & Artists*, June 1971, pp. 20–23. I developed Edward Hyams's concept of the French garden as a 'roofless room' in relation to Lassus's work.

Danish Mission Boat

SK[2]

--- for it happens that, when I was on one of my fourteen year old (?) Wartime tours of Britain, I stayed – innocently enough – with SK's girl friend Milein (spelling?) in Oxford . . . and I once had coffee with that other girl (the fast one) in some Oxford café . . . At least I think it was Oxford. In those days, travelling a great deal (as I did), and the Nation being in the state that it was, I was not always clear as to my whereabouts (the Signs had been removed as a precaution against Parachutists), and Oxford and Cambridge were much the same to me. Around the same time, and in the same town, I stayed – also innocently – with Bryan Winter's girl friend; I am pretty sure it was Cambridge, no, Oxford. The Slade School was there, too, at that time. I am sorry to say that I did not meet SK. I was actually arrested as a suspected Parachutist (Sprackenzeedoytch?) and sent back to Scotland, after interrogation. (I remember that my suitcase, when it was searched, was found to contain The Selected Poems of Lorca, and The Romantic Agony – this last purchased in Zwemmers, from the very hand of the (in)famous Friedman (spelling?), sometimes known as 'The Count'. At that time, in Zwemmers, one could expect to be served either by The Count, or by the poet Ruthven Todd (who I knew as Ruthven Snow).[3] The person who was most charming to me at the time, was Mr Spender, who took me to Lyons Corner House and treated me to large and London-y cakes. The very first thing I did when I arrived in London – which was actually upon a large torpedo – (I had boarded the lorry in the dark, near Birmingham, after leaving a transport café which was surrounded by police, seeking a Deserter, who was inside) – was to call at Horizon's office, to see CC. Luckily (as it was only dawn and the Firewatchers had not yet departed) he had not arrived: but the lady who later married George Orwell, came and let me in, and was very friendly and benign . . . This is quite enough of my reminisces. And I have got a long way from Keyes . . . .

I will be writing a proper letter ere long. Meanwhile I hope you are fine, and that Holland lived up to its romantic horizons . . . .

2. Sidney Keyes's initials suggest the Skaggerrak, a strait running between the Jutland peninsula of Denmark and the coasts of Sweden and Norway.

3. This is a play on words, involving the correct pronunciation of the Scottish name Ruthven as 'Riven': Ruthven Snow/Driven Snow. Mario Praz's celebrated study, *The Romantic Agony*, first published in Italy in 1930, had been issued in an English translation in 1933.

(as I seem to remember they looked from the troop train, in my old troop train days).

--- Your old troop trainer,

Ian

These autobiographical remarks touched off by the name of Sidney Keyes cast a flood of light on Finlay's experience as a very young man in wartime Britain. Finlay had left his school in Glasgow at the age of fourteen, but it is hardly conceivable that the journeys and connections that he mentions took place when he was around that age, that is, in 1940–41.The meeting that he mentions, not with Keyes himself but with Keyes's girlfriend, Milein Cosmann, is perhaps indicative of the likely date. Keyes entered the army in Northern Ireland in April 1942, and was commissioned in the Queen's Own West Kent Regiment in September of the same year, leaving for active service in March 1943. It seems probable that 1942–43 was the period during which Finlay stayed, in his absence, with Milein Cosmann.

This visit would, indeed, have taken place not in Cambridge but in Oxford, where the Slade School of Art had been evacuated from the outset of the Second World War. The landscape painter Bryan Wynter, later to be associated with the St Ives School, was studying at the Slade from 1938 to 1940, both in London and, after the move, in Oxford. As a conscientious objector, he remained in the area to work on land drainage in Oxfordshire.

The various London references also ring true for a date around 1942/43. Anton Zwemmer's bookshop in the Charing Cross Road already served at the time as a meeting place for the London art world. The Scottish poet, Ruthven Todd (1914–78), who was a conscientious objector during the war, could well have been employed there, and doubtless his writings were already known to Finlay. Cyril Connolly (C.C.) was editing the literary magazine Horizon *from 1940 onwards, and he employed the 'Euston Road Venus', Sonia Brownell (the future Sonia Orwell) as his secretary and editorial assistant. Lyons Corner House, either the Strand or the Tottenham Court Road branch, would have been just the place for Stephen Spender to entertain an aspiring, but hungry, young writer to tea and cakes.*

The 'proper letter', to which Finlay alludes at the close of these fascinating recollections, was never in fact written. Our earlier grumbles about difficulties with the postal service, whether these were due to inefficiency or adverse weather conditions, had anticipated the eventual breakdown of discussions about a possible pay rise between the workforce and the management. A postal strike was declared, and it began on 20 January. It was to last until 4 March.

This was the longest period since our correspondence began in the autumn of 1964 over which we were unable to exchange regular letters. My own occupation with a number of extra-curricular activities during the interval of over six weeks is made clear in the letter that follows. Finlay's publications had continued to build up over the same period, and they were now ready for distribution. His new post-card 'The Harbour', with a photograph by Diane Tammes, was sent to me on 15 March, with a brief message. It was followed only a day later by the card (designed by Michael Harvey) which was devised to remind Finlay's correspondents of a letter that was due: 'The Sign of the Nudge'. By then my own letter of reply had already been sent off.

Canterbury
16 March 1971

Dear Ian,

I am really having to take a firm hold on my wayward instincts in order to set pen to paper – after that curious period of subterfuge which I can hardly imagine to be past. Will these suspicious stamps really carry my letter to its destination?[4] One simply has to take it on trust, as the Post has ceased to be one of the certainties of life & become a mere probability – dear me!

At any rate, I can vouch for the arrival of your two very welcome poems. Both the ketch and the harbouring yacht are splendid – just right. And I have even eventually received my copies of the folder from Sunderland.[5] It is a useful package with which to overwhelm friends – they take to it as to a Christmas stocking.

I wonder if you have had a pleasant winter/spring? It has hardly escaped my notice that quantities of snow descended on the Lowlands from time to time. Here we have been relatively unscathed, & the occasional Kentish avalanche has been brushed away before the day was out. My term has been grouped around various activities of a mysteriously interconnected kind – that might fall into the headings a) silent Films b) Epitaphs & c) Beowulf.

4. The transition to decimal currency had coincided with the postal strike, and stamps were accordingly inscribed 3P instead of 5d.

5. The Ceolfrith folder, including several photographs by Diane Tammes and my essay on 'Ian Hamilton Finlay: Engineer and Bricoleur'. This had ostensibly been posted in November of the previous year.

As for the first, I have fulfilled a former project of gathering together 12 or so people every fortnight to see the inexhaustibly rich treasures of the 1920's. Nothing but the whirring of the reels & the occasional gasp of ecstasy disturbs our attentive response to, say, Garbo's first major screen role in the *Atonement of Gosta Berling*;[6] or indeed to Doktor Kraftt & Leni Riefenstahl stuck on a freezing ledge in *White Hell of Pitz Palu*.[7]

Epitaphs are a more private occupation, pursued only with the friend who previously distinguished himself in the recollection of Classical love stories. We have collected in Canterbury & surrounding villages a series of fine haunting epitaphs that are so badly weather-beaten & scarred that they are in danger of disappearing for ever (this type of verse never seems to be found in good repair, or inside a church). We employ a variety of analytical and actual tools, from textual conjectures to garden hoes, & not long ago deciphered, for example, by candlelight the following dignified and weighty lines from St Dunstan's Churchyard itself[8] (candlelight restores the lettering marvellously by casting oblique light on the indentations):

> Hearken ye young, ye hoary sires attend
> Hear all who breathe the ashes of a Friend.
> To you they speak, on you benign they call,
> Heirs of the tomb and partners of the Fall!
> Return (they cry) to earth, return again,
> He bids who made for mocks the sons of men.
> But can you view – & can you thoughtless read
> This kind alarm? This summons from the dead?
> Can you unmoved the general sentence hear
> Nor sigh one sigh, nor shed one genuine tear?
> In vain if so would worlds entomb'd arise
> To rouse your fears or point you to the skies.

The interest, I think, is less in any absolute achievement than in the context: in the total anonymity of the work, in its direct appeal to the reader & in its almost complete effacement (to the extent of being half buried in the ground). But it is also fascinating, isn't it, to note the persistence of an almost 17th century sensibility in a mid-18th c. inscription?

6. Directed by Mauritz Stiller (1924).

7. Directed by Arnold Fanck and Georg Wilhelm Pabst (1929): Krafft is the fictional hero, and Riefenstahl the actress who plays his wife.

8. The churchyard of St Dunstan's was situated immediately over the wall of my back garden.

Finally to *Beowulf* (that must have seemed the most eccentric of all). I sponsored a splendid performance of the said epic in the college last Friday – by almost life-size puppets in the Japanese idiom. The company managed to keep 80 squashed people spell-bound for over two hours & three monsters were decisively put paid to.[9]

Now I am retiring rapidly from this scene of too frantic activity to a quiet fortnight in Venice, as I did last year. In case you can trust the Italian postal service with a letter, my address will be: Pensione alla Salute da Cici
Dorsoduro
Venice
I shall be there till just before Easter, & shall be spending the weekend of Easter itself up in Yorkshire.

Have you heard anything of the Los Angeles production going forward?[10] It would be nice to know that was happening. My communications with America are reopened, & it seems that [*The Tradition of*]*Constructivism* is not far behind. I am now thinking up the most fiendish diagrams to demonstrate the inter-relatedness of aspects of the field. I have one which goes like this:

Other names to be filled in presently.

Very best wishes & love to Sue, Eck & Ailie
Yours

Stephen

9. Described as 'an interpretation of the early English Epic' by Lawrence Butler, this play was presented to around 80 guests on 12 March in the Upper Senior Common Room of Rutherford College. It involved puppets and masked puppeteers in the style of the Japanese 'Bunraku' theatre.

10. *Honey by the Water*, in press with the Black Sparrow Press, Los Angeles, but subject to prolonged delays.

Stonypath
22 March 1971

Dear Stephen,

I was most pleased to have your letter today. Like you, I still find the postal service anything but credible, and it would scarcely be too much to say that nothing can ever be quite the same again. Or as Democritus had it, (or someone), You cannot step out of a postal strike the man you stepped in. All unbeknown to you, our phone, too, was bust: so for virtually all the strike we were entirely cut off from the outside world. We had no sooner adjusted to this, than Mr Jackson signalled defeat by shaking his large and sad moustache.[11]

And while we were having our strike, they were having their earthquake . . . which, as it happens, reduced the machinery which was to print 'A Sailor's Calendar', to rubble. Fortunately, it seems that all the Something Else Press people were spared. And Black Sparrow was either more remote, or is less sensitive, for it has sent only a nonchalant postcard, talking of 'interruptions'. (What is a Disaster for Dick Higgins, is an interruption for Seamus Cooney . . to whom I had meanwhile sent an enquiring postcard, couched in Apocalyptic terms . . .)

I must say that we missed you, and indeed – as a result, I am sure, of your silent film sessions, I had a whoppingly awful, and endless, dream, in one reel of which I encountered you at an absolutely awful London party: you were just leaving in the company of a sixty-year old heiress (symbolising The Arts Council of Great Britain?) . . and it was being whispered that you were, secretly, a famous hurdler. We left this awful party in the same cab, but as you were firmly dedicated to the company of the heiress – and I was, myself, with a girl – I do not know what happened to you. (I know what happened to me and it is a jolly good thing I woke up about reel 23).

After being out of touch with you since the start of the strike, or, since about Christmas 1941, it seems rather impossible to even attempt to catch up with The News. I must mention that we had one incredible afternoon, in which Christopher Carrell arrived with his usual retinue of unexplained followers (men, women, and children), at the same time as the Carnwath Film Society,

11. The moustachioed Tom Jackson was General Secretary of the Union of Post Office Workers, which had called the postal strike.

which was bent on borrowing Serpolette[12] to act a donkey of the time of The Crusades, on the Moorish hill behind our house. Christopher Carrell, as you will know, always dresses like a Mohican: while the Carnwath chemist had dressed himself in a suit* [*medieval, Moorish] made of sacks: they met at our gate.

I was delighted with the epitaph you sent me. I have a nice (old) book on epitaphs which I must let you read in bed when next you are here. It is very comprehensive.

Your sample diagram for 'Constructivism' is giving me a lot of pleasure. The one (or bit, or triangle) marked Gabo, is in a very perilous position, like that of someone dangling from the top of a high pyramid . . . and if I was Gabo I would consider a return to a more academic mode, without delay. I am sure, yes, that it is a semiotic diagram: it must be. Let me warn you that I am preparing for the printer, a postcard which will end semioticism for ever, (collapse of stout diagram). (I am also preparing a 'Homage to Donald McGill' postcard, which I will make every effort to post to you while you are in Yorkshire . . so that your mother will know what frightful friends you have.)[13]

Have you seen the new Tarasque? It has a poem of yours in it[14] – and more misprints than I have ever seen in a little magazine: one would not have thought it possible. Stuart [Mills] explained that it has double the number of misprints because it is a double-number: to which I retorted that I was doubly-sure I had been right to say (a few months ago) that I would never, never, never publish with Tarasque again. Statements like: The concrete peotpiysperticularatenttion to the exastence of langauge on the pgae – are peculiarly perturbing. Moreover one would think

[letter resumed on a new sheet of writing paper on 3 April]

12. Serpolette, the name of the Finlays' donkey, was derived from the stories of the French author, Alphonse Daudet. The French word *serpolet* means wild thyme.

13. In the event, this 'Happy Holiday Postcard' was sent to me in Canterbury on 2 July 1971. The image is a blue rectangle, and the text reads: 'William and Rose with their briefs down'.

> pl. 18

14. 'Vierzehnheiligen (the) (three) (ovals) of Balthasar Neumann', shortly to be a poem card published by Tarasque Press. The allusion is to the Bavarian Rococo church by Neumann, dedicated to 'fourteen saints', the nave of which forms three consecutive, broken ovals as observed in the ground plan. See Nikolaus Pevsner, *An Outline of European Architecture.* (Harmondsworth: Penguin, 1964 reprint), pp. 187–88.

[Stonypath]
Society for the Protection of the Arts against the Arts Council
3 April 1971

Dear Stephen,

but what, moreover, one would think . . . we shall never know. I really despair of getting this letter finished, for each time I clear a wee space, it is filled by some other, intrusive, energy-diverting problem . . . and I will never be able to send you the message I had hoped to send --- to Venice -----

BEWARE OF THE DOGE

(I hope he didn't get you.)

Do you like this splendid new paper? It is what I use for writing to The Arts Council, and Lord Eccles, on. I also use it for my controversies with the Scottish Branch of PEN, and The National Library of Scotland. This weekend I am starting a new society, (rather specially for **PEN**), **PAN**, (The Association of Garden-Poets, incorporating **PICK**). From time to time, I send them all a Sign of the Nudge, just to keep them up to scratch.

The other day we had a call from London, on a very poor line. I thought it claimed to be Mr Carr, but it turned out to be The Parliamentary Commissioner, whose representative called to see me on April Fools Day. With a great effort of restraint, I refrained from shooting him with a water-pistol, and shouting **APRIL FOOL HA HA**. He was in fact a rather nice wee soul, and he amused us with long stories about **MINTEC** (the government-sponsored peppermint) and The Strange Case of The Green Honey – a story which I, in my turn, retailed to Sue's Uncle – who for some reason turned white with fury half-way through. To get back to the point, the **PC**'s representative, was quite hopeful about Le Grand Fulcrum Affair, and had a splendid file of evidence which – I must say – did seem quite to dispose of Eccles and Goodman. To my great joy, an Unknown Hero in The British Museum had given it as his opinion that the Fulcrum editions could not – either legally or in terms of publishing practice – be considered first editions. This is the **ONLY** man in an official position who has ever been brave enough to **FACE** that question with an unequivocal answer. Anyway, if only the **PC** finds in my favour – which is not of course certain, for it is not a departmental decision, but his alone – I will then try to have my **MP** raise the real question: Why have Goodman and Eric White, and the London lawyers with the London book dealers, assumed the right to re-write the Law on first editions.

You may not realise that the Arts Council has been openly advocating a theory of first editions, which would not only contradict traditional practice, but would make it impossible, in twenty years time, to say whether a book belonged to a particular decade, far less a year . . . with the most unfortunate results for critics and any kind of scholarship.

.

Well now, dear Stephen, when you were here you made a little **ACTION LIST**. Could I perhaps refer you to that, and offer the hope that we might clear some things up. May I number these . .?

1. What shall we do about Mr Karpel? Our box of offerings must be sitting, unexplained – and inexplicable – in the museum . . . It would be nice if we could get back our shipment costs . . but nicer still if Mr Karpel would be in touch, and would buy a decent selection of things. As I recall, you were going to send him the Sunderland catalogue (which took such a strangely long time to meander from Sunderland to Kent: it is those weedy canals).

2. You were going to write to Ships Monthly,* [*And what of that French magazine?] about doing a posh article on me. I am encouraged in this possibility by the curious fact that the January Editorial was entirely devoted to the well-known ship, John Keats. (Incidentally, The Director of The National Maritime Museum was well pleased with the little Hobah/ketch leaflet/poem, and has written requesting to purchase 100 (sic) copies.)

3. The Last of The Mohicans, Mr Carrell, has now got a substantial sum of money for my proposed retrospective show in January (travelling to Newcastle, Stirling, and elsewhere). I believe he has around £1000, which has to be divided between travelling expenses, the completion of a small film, and so on, and so on . . . But, as you know, I have always made it a point to say that the chief purpose of this money must be, to produce a catalogue which is really a small book – a catalogue which will remain of interest after the exhibition, and which may be sold in bookshops. The point is this, Stephen. Mr Carrell is a little vague, or should one say contemporary, and if we are going to produce this catalogue/book it must be taken into our own hands. I have found, in Stellar Press, a printer who is (apparently) both willing to attempt a decent standard of printing, and to charge for it at a reasonable (or possible) rate. The question then is, what do you and I wish to do. Mr

> Carrell knows I would like you to write the catalogue. He is agreeable. You and I must **NOW** decide what we would like, exactly, and press for that with a strong undeviating single-mindedness. As soon as we have decided between us, I will ask Mr Carrell to be in touch with you, directly.

The question is, would you like to write the catalogue yourself . . or would you prefer that it was a matter of (say) three essays, involving 2 other people as well? My personal feeling would be, that I would love if you did it, and we could have a chance to do a definitive, well-printed bit of work . . using photos of the garden-poems and illustrations of poem/prints etc. What I see is the kind of book which could be stocked by Wittenborn for years to come . . and sold in Zwemmers . . But it is largely a question of **OUR** deciding what we want to do, and of seeing that it is done.

Could you have a wee think, Stephen. I will listen most carefully to anything you suggest.

I have several new garden-poems which you must see before too long. And an almost <u>undue</u> amount of projects in hand, or printers' hands, or the indelicate hands of far-off people . . . I need a good chat with you.

Anyway. One last request for the moment: Could you keep your eye open for a book which would be a kind of counterpart to that delightful Panofsky essay . . A book – **THERE MUST** be such a book – which deals with the **IDEA** of the elegaic [sic] tradition . . . . . in paintings or gardens or literature.

I hope you are fine. Write soon. Forgive the tone of this letter which tries to deal with too much, too quickly . . .

Love,

Ian

Canterbury
21 April 1971

Dear Ian,

Here I am writing once again on the egregious paper of *20th Century Studies*. It may as well signify that I am back again in business with that particular outfit, having organised a Symposium or <u>Colloque</u> on the 'nouveau roman' for a week on Saturday.[15] We shall be rejoicing in the presence of Michel Butor, but shall not, unfortunately, be attracting Pinget (which is a great pity, as **PONGE** is visiting London that very weekend . . .). I shall be in the Chair, which should be rather fascinating, as it seems unclear whether one ('On') will be speaking French or English. I am irresistibly tempted to use the formula employed in the better sort of Western for identifying successive speakers:

'The Chair recognises its old friend, the Honble. Major Cassius Harbuckle (or other).'[16]

It was splendid to hear you the other evening, & I do reaffirm my enthusiasm for the catalogue/book. On mature reflection, the idea of the personal appreciations of I.H.F. sounds too awesome to be true. There would have to be a serious stipulation that each was to be accompanied by an appreciation in the other direction, so to speak. Or a thumb-nail sketch. . . .

Yes, I really must write to *Ships Monthly*, which project was overtaken by the great freeze. I must also send the catalogue to Karpel – it just arrived a day or two before I was claimed by Italy. I shall certainly make a point of stressing the payment for the shipment costs, as he did definitely guarantee that.

As for *L'Oeil*, I was assailed by great doubts as to whether the photographs alone would get across to the French editorial people, especially as they <u>pretend</u> to know a good deal more English than they in fact do. I decided that I should certainly try to provide some linking material in French, rather than rely on the Sunderland essay.

How interesting about the Parliamentary Commissioner & the unknown hero of the British Museum! What exactly will it amount to if he finds in your favour? What sort of humble pie will Ld. Goodman have to eat?

Everything is very summer-like here, & I am buying things for the garden in anticipation of lots of time here. I am also fitting up a kind of impromptu cutting room, since the gathering of epitaphs has resulted in an eventual film (or so it will be when it is cut). It is (will be) a film of great austerity,

15. This symposium took place on 1 May. Michel Butor attended, and the interview that Guido Almansi and I conducted with him, after a good dinner, was published in the special issue of *20th Century Studies*, 'Directions in the nouveau roman' (December 1971).

16. Major Cassius Starbuckle (acted by John Cannadine) plays a minor role in John Ford's Western, *The Man Who Shot Liberty Valance* (1962).

concentrating almost exclusively on dignified tombstones, which remain almost completely static. There will also be strange misty shots of Kentish landscape with the odd flurry of sea-gulls.

Funnily enough (!) I have not seen the new Tarasque & consequently am a bit puzzled about the poem by me in it. It must be a poem about Boudin, I should say, since I occasionally write the odd poem about Boudin & send it to Simon (Boudin is, as the French say, inépuisable). Which odd poem it is, will have to be seen.

That reminds me that the very day of the great postal interregnum a letter from Stuart reached me about a possible reference for a job in the Lakes. I never wrote the reference as the people never asked me for it. Do you know if it fell through completely? I think it was the Kendal Arts Centre.

I must make sure to come up to Stonypath during the summer, to see the new things & to prepare the book in more detail. Probably late August would be a good time, or late September. In July I am beginning a series of south-wending stays at St Aubin, Jersey, where friends have recently bought a house overlooking the old port. I wonder what they fish for in Jersey?

I must return to my 'nouveaux romans' for a while & cook up the relevant speculations on 'Narrative & discontinuity'.

Love to Sue, Eck & Ailie,
Yours

Stephen

PS. Gabo is in fact in a much more secure position than Tatlin, who really is at the end of his tether by the base of the second triangle – it all shows how the diagram can lie.

Stonypath
24 April 1971

Dear Stephen,

it was really delightful to get your letter; no-one writes like you do. There are so few letters which make me laugh – and so many which might make me cry, if it wasn't for my superb self-control.

I thought you might like this green-headed paper for a change. I have decided that, as my letters fetch more than my books, it may be a good idea to begin to treat the letter-page as the work of art . . . and the poem/print as a mere extra, or postscript.

I wrote to Christmas Carol and told him of our plans for the monograph. He has not yet replied and will shortly get a Nudge. Given that he is unreliable, (as who – except you – under 35, is not), he is sometimes surprisingly trustworthy.

Yes, do write to Ships Monthly. The latest editorial is (again) devoted to Keats, and contrives to allude to Dylan Thomas – "Dylan" to SM. – The question may well be whether the Wild Hawthorn is avant-garde enough.

Please try, too, to write the 'linkage' material for L'Oeil.

Talking of oil, and linkage material, our dam is now almost free from pollution – and we have actually installed the projected bridge, leading to the new island. It would be untrue to say that it is Watteauesque, but it certainly something which one would not have thought the Pentagon – the Pentlands, capable of, until now. A white bridge, lacking only Munch Maidens, in little white dresses and straw-hats, pensively regarding the water. – On the island there are – or will be any day now, flowers called periwinkles. And there are already three alder trees. During the winter I will devise a poem for this prize site.

I'm afraid that any Victory, via The Parliamentary Commissioner, (who I seem to have entangled in the rigging, as well as in my argument), must be a small one. You see, his area of reference is very restricted, and he cannot, in fact, even comment on the doings of The Arts Council, as that is not a government department. On the other hand, his department does seem to take an honest look at the evidence, and after two years of deliberate lies and dishonesty, the fact that the PC would send someone to The British Museum to look at the editions of my book, is, well, joyous for Sue and I . . and very generally encouraging. We will now have to wait and see what his report actually says. What it cannot do, is to say anything directly about Goodman or Fulcrum: it must confine itself to their present mouthpiece, Eccles.[17]

17. Viscount Eccles was Minister for the Arts in the Heath government from 1970 to 1973, and had declined to intervene in the 'Fulcrum Affair'. Lord Goodman was Chairman of the Arts Council of Great Britain.

My hope is that I could then proceed to widen this first little hole in their horrid wall (or web).

You must tell Sue what you have been buying for your garden. She goes in for plants and things. As you know, my own view is – as usual – the traditional one: that the proper materials of gardening are water, trees, and grass.

I am delighted ---- do you realise that I am answering your letter in its order? ---- that you are making the Epitaph Film. I have a splendid idea: arising from the fact that, when Jessie [Sheeler] was here, I hired a projectionist to show my terrible Arts Council film – no their terrible Arts Council film – in our sittingroom. If I manage to finish 'Fifties and Zulus', and you finish 'Goodbye To All That' --- is it called? – we could have a special film-show when you visit us: that would be jolly nice.

I like your sentence about the 'dignified tombstones' which 'remain almost completely static'. If it had been an Arts Council film, they would have insisted on undignified tomb stones, waving wildly about.

The least I can do is to send you Tarasque; you will scarcely see it, otherwise. – As for whether Stuart got that job, or not, who knows? He asked me about the reference too, but I heard no more. He and Simon grow worse and worse about communication – and indeed, Jessie [Sheeler] told me that she has three times written to Tarasque, asking to buy their publications, and has not had a reply.

"I wonder what they fish for in Jersey?"

Wool.

.

Yes, that will be lovely if you come up in August or September. We will look forward to that.

I will keep your indoor sundial for you. As a matter of fact, I have a crate of them, as the Arts Council, with its usual efficiency, has not even bothered to collect them, far less to do anything about selling the 75, or 200, or whatever it was, they asked me to supply. Perhaps I should confiscate them.

Your Tarasque poem is not about Boudin. But I do find it obscure. Now that you know which one it is, you can explain it to me.[18] (The factual basis: the

18. See note 14, p. 120.

poem I will be entirely capable of understanding, I am sure). (In that sort of way I am a pleasant change.)

When you write to Mr Karpel, try to give him a sharp reminder about actually buying our things. Indeed his most sensible course (you might say) would be to send someone over to Stonypath, to meet me, and to see the (assorted) works. I am feeling very disillusioned with art museums, as even the Stedelijk turns out not to answer letters in a business-like way – and they have not (as they promised) paid me for my specially prepared work. No doubt they will, but I get tired of slapdash modernity.

Did you notice that Sir K. Clark calls Cythera 'Cytherea'?[19] Perhaps he supposes that is posh?

Ah dear Cytherea
Land of hysteria
Where the wisteria
Grows . . . .

– I expect you know that old song?

·

I have just corrected the colour proofs of a delightful little card (folded) which I am doing with Ian Gardner. I am not sure what Period it takes off . . . Perhaps it is one I am in the process of inventing, a kind of imaginary amalgam of [Maurice] Denis, [Charles Rennie] Mackintosh, Kate Greenaway, Seurat, and The Architypal [sic] Children's Book. In this Land and Time, not only the tombstones but even the trees, remain dignified and almost completely static. There is a magical, almost monochrome Light (caused in part by the strictest economy in the use of printers' blocks).[20]

You will be delighted to learn that I addressed a letter to:

The Tug Department,
National Maritime Museum,
Greenwich

19. The translation of the title of Watteau's famous painting as 'Embarkation to Cytherea' dates back as far as the eighteenth century, and was still generally in use in the earlier part of the twentieth century.

20. This description fits the folding card *Tree-Shells* (1971, with Ian Gardner), sent to me on 16 July 1971.

and received a reply. (I am seeking reference material for a postcard to be subtitled 'Homage to Tarasque Press').

Love,

Ian

Swan Hotel
Lavenham
Suffolk
23 May 1971

Dear Ian,

Here I am meditating about the quality of Englishness. First of all, it occurred to me as a result of a visit this afternoon to some (retired) friends at the magnificently named Booty Hall in this vicinity.[21] The garden, as the creator proudly explained, is divided up into five successive rectangles, each divided from the other by a massive flower border, row of fruit trees or other barrier. So each area, of curving turf, grass-framed lily pool, or paved enclosure sprouting with rock plants & herbs, is an autonomous space. The whole is bound together by paths leading along the ancient red wall (festooned with clematis, honeysuckle & lilac) that encloses three sides of the garden.

It is like William Morris's prescription for the Red House – winding paths opening into episodic open spaces (the pattern of 'Concerning Geoffrey Maltête'[22] also).

It recalls me to this very time last weekend, when I was at a house in Surrey of a slightly grander variety – adjusted by Sir E. Lutyens.[23] There the long

21. Neville and Winifred Sykes had moved from a Georgian house adjacent to Thorpe Grange, my parents' first home in Almondbury, West Yorkshire, to this seventeenth-century hall in rural Suffolk.

22. 'Concerning Geoffrey Teste Noire' is a poem which nests one narrative within another, being spoken ostensibly by an informant of the historian Jean Froissart. It is included in William Morris's first collection, *The Defence of Guenevere* (1858). I used an extract from another poem in this collection, 'A Garden by the Sea', as an epigraph in my essay for Finlay's 1972 catalogue.

23. Lutyens had worked at Littleworth Cross, at the time of this letter the home of Sir John and Lady Gutch, at Seale near Guildford. This was also where Lutyens first met his future collaborator, the garden designer, Gertrude Jekyll.

stately pathways between flowering rhododendrons – occasionally parting to reveal a billiard-smooth croquet lawn – entirely deprived one of any sense of wider spatial reference & landed one at the front door as if at the focus of a maze (the front door itself being set exquisitely at an angle to the corner of the building, as if slicing off the abrupt intrusion of geometry).

Then once again I have been reading Kipling assiduously & almost for the first time. I have mainly taken the middle and later stories which I find entrancing. Without making a specific reference, I find it so subtly pleasurable to be led on by Kipling, into a space of suggestion whose formal outlines dissolve and reform quite unaccountably until the final order sets everything to rights – yet leaves the mystery of the journey that has been undertaken.[24]

I think I would only be able to define this group of impressions as the discovery of English space, & it is making me realise with curious intensity a kind of insistence in what I had perhaps taken for granted. I must also send you on that count the small volume of poems of the friend with whom I made the Churchyard film – who is very much responsible for showing me what is in Kipling. They have some of the uncertainty of youth, but some of the certainty which I suspect you would recognise.

It would be/will be delightful to show you the Churchyard film. It is in places quite breathtaking, as it has both the formal beauty of these gracefully ageing stones & the pathos of texts almost obliterated & lost. The film is simply a means through which the stones speak, & that, as their texts declare, is what they are meant to do.

All this tends to drive to a different place news of M[ichel] Butor (known scathingly by his French literary enemies as 'New Zealand Butor') – but that can come at another time, since M. Butor certainly incarnates to the highest degree the quality of being incroyablement French.

I will write again at a smaller lapse of time & of course thank you in more detail for the splendid Macmillan poems.[25]

Love to Sue, Eck & Ailie,   Yours Stephen

24. The collections of short stories which interested me principally at this time were *Traffics and Discoveries* (1904), *Debits and Credits* (1926) and *Limits and Renewals* (1932).

25. *Poems to Hear and See* (New York: Macmillan, 1971).

Stonypath
27 May 1971

Dear Stephen,

it was nice to hear you on the 'phone. You are one of those people who always sound very immediate and there on the 'phone; there is a great presence in your voice. Perhaps you should become A Radio Critic?

Here is the 'Seashells' rough. You can imagine it in a folder, akin to that of the Vuillard folder. Then we could either print the little essay somewhere on the folder, or on a sheet the same size as the print itself. I do think a very short essay will be quite adequate . . and indeed I suppose that 'essay' is not the word. Introduction would be more like the thing.

As you will see the boat-hulls – which are known as 'shells' in the building-world – are presented as if they are shells, brought together by a collector. Ian Proctor, (I enclose an article on him, for your guidance),[26] is a little disconcerted that the 'shells' are rendered in positions which boats would scarcely take up: but this is (of course) because he is thinking of them as boats and not as seashells. The introduction might mention this aspect – that the seashell came (as it were) first, though the 'substance' of the image is the stuff of boats (as it were).

Another point you might refer to, is that of the special place of the seashell in European culture . . . And I suppose you might say something about the place of the 'sign' in my recent work (thus giving various people A NUDGE). I have my usual hope that the print might appeal to boat-people – a non-specialist audience . . (which rather means, doesn't it, an audience which specialises in other things?)

You will realise that my own excitement about this poem/print stems from my delight in connecting things, and there is of course a special delight in having obtained the collaboration of the leading chap in the particular area: you know how sadly unimaginative people are when it comes to collaborating – see, e.g. architects and concrete poetry. I think the 'avant-garde' is pretty unimaginative too, for when it seeks to establish connections it rarely perceives natural-aesthetic ones, but prefers the strained and tenuous (to say the least!).

26. The article enclosed had been published in *Yachts and Yachting*, 26 February 1971, pp. 526–57.

Perhaps your introduction could add a reference to the aid rendered by the good Ron Costley.

But really Stephen, in essence, all that is needed is a short, translucent, pale pink introduction, such as may help the moderately-intelligent yachtsman to appreciate (i.e. enjoy) the print.

You will note my use of the singular in that sentence: I never exaggerate (spelling?) the sales-potential of the Wild Hawthorn poem/print.

Love,

Ian

En route
6 June 1971

Dear Ian,

Just a quick note written vaguely close to Charing X, to accompany the pink text. I hope it is O.K. & leave it to you of course to make any necessary connections. The paste-up has been despatched to Ron C.

Love to all,
Yours

Stephen

[Enclosure]

Ian Hamilton Finlay is a poet who works not only with words, but with the whole range of signs that man employs for the purposes of communication. The point of departure for his activity over the past decade was the international movement of concrete poetry. But the works which he is undertaking at present owe very little to that tradition. He makes use of very diverse types of sign, drawn from different areas of nature and culture. Often the articulation of these signs requires the collaboration of specialists from particular areas of art and design. But the central intention is always to create a unified whole, which draws upon the common iconographic treasury of Western art and literature.

'Seashells' is a clear example of this new direction. Finlay has harnessed the talents of Ian Proctor, one of the leading British boat designers, in addition to the typographic skills of Ron Costley. He presents the designer's sketched hulls, or 'shells', as if they were a group of seashells mounted in a collector's case. In this way, the two different types of object, from different orders of being, are identified in a single figure: as we would describe it in a literary context, a metaphor is established.

Obviously the effectiveness of 'Seashells' depends on the degree to which this identification releases an additional charge of meaning. The metaphor must 'seem right', although there may be no precise way of explaining the effect. It might be worth underlining in this case that the opposition between boat and seashell is mediated by the use of a simple, diagrammatic form. The disproportion between two orders of size is negated by the fact that the boat only appears as a blueprint (at which stage its linear patterning provides a close analogy to the whorls of the shell). It might also be worth referring to at least one precedent from the History of Western Art. Does not Botticelli's Venus arise from the waves in a boat that is also a shell? The purpose of Finlay's work is to explore these various areas of aesthetic experience, to equate the metaphor and the model, to reestablish the context of the traditional motif, and so to reconstruct from fragmentary pieces the fabric of Classicism.[27]

Stonypath
16 June 1971

Dear Stephen,

your Introduction for 'Seashells' was splendid; in fact, I had scarcely expected that even you could manage anything so concise and elegant. It is now (I trust) with Ron Costley, and you will see the finished folder as soon as a large Shenval wave, drops the lot upon my shore.

Thank you very much indeed.

The Year is wheeching by, and already the hour of Michael Harvey's visit (a week today) to construct the 2 giant sundials, is upon us. I have been making arrangements for the concrete, sand, colouring, steel mesh, and goodness knows what-all materials of Ian Hamilton Pharos[28] (spelling?) Trade. As luck will have it, Michaels 5-day visit seems certain to coincide with the reappearance of the Macauley Bulldozers, not seen at Stonypath since the

27. This is the text that was printed, with slight emendations, in the 'Seashells' folder.

28. The Pharos (lighthouse) of Alexandria was one of the Seven Wonders of the Ancient World.

days of The Biggar Sundial, (soon to be only second Biggar). Several large men came and took measurements on the site of the proposed loch. Promising to return in late-June with the appropriate machines.

Meanwhile, I have become enamoured of battleships. For some intricate reason I never noticed these beautiful objects before.

I will soon be surprising you with several new postcards and cards.

In December I am having – in the R. Demarco Gallery – my first exhibition of poems in neon-light. I have found a splendid neon-technician, and my first little neon-poem, barque, is already almost complete. The new ones are considerably more ambitious, and should be superb.

I also contemplate an exhibition of the neon-technician's drawings for the works, as these are of a very high quality. Perhaps I will convert them into screen prints.

As regards several practical matters:

1. Christopher Carrell should be in touch with you about the catalogue/monograph, which will have to be ready for the printer rather sooner than I had first thought.

2. Perhaps I should just write to the editor of 'Ships Monthly' myself, sending material?

3. The photos and the French magazine. Perhaps you are too busy to attempt this, and it would be more practical if I sent the photos to someone else, and they could then approach the magazine? What do you think, Stephen?

4. The Karpel Question. I am not quite sure where we stand on this. I feel the Question is, in fact, lying untended somewhere about Doncaster. Could we make a last effort to sort it out?

Mary Ellen [Solt] writes sad letters about the proposed Museum of Modern Art, (**MOMA**), show of concrete, and the awful machinations (quite Tinguely) of Designers, (Designs of Designers?), and clashes of rival cliques, and letters of Enticement to Embargo . . . How nice it is to be Away From It All.

Did I tell you that I have begun a series of glass net-float poems? This is the finally proper material base for the self-sufficient fragment. Love from your self-insufficient

Ian

Canterbury
17 June 1971

Dear Ian,

I was very glad to hear that the 'Seashells' introduction was suitable. It is a realisation that I am greatly looking forward to.

Here I am just at the point of peeping over the next hedge (week) & seeing the long lush vacation. It has reached the stage where I am engaged in saying the same thing, with variations, to six pairs of persons for one hour each virtually on running (running is the right word). The fact that the thing is, say, Neo-classicism, only just redeems the activity. Still, the strawberries are with us now, & the voice of the sea-trout is heard in the land. So my exhausting days are at least punctuated by long gastronomic evenings.

Do you remember that in my last letter I mentioned the imminent arrival of a book of poems? Here it is. Quite a lot of the work is not likely to appeal to you, I would think. But what I find encouraging about it is that the symbols, & the recurrent images, have a real hold. They are not, so to speak, generated as a product of self-expression. They are attained, in their separateness.[29]

I have evolved a third, as well as a second, poem/card. Did I ever really explain *Vierzehnheiligen*?[30] That is, I suppose, about the enclosure of paradaisical space – & so is the next, which refers more particularly to the English tradition:

> pl. 18

The Garden as a parenthesis

[ ]

Ref: William Morris's 'long walks & trellis-enclosed flower-plots.'

29. See note 34.

30. See note 15.

That is the substance, but colour and planning will add piquancy. I am trying to see the garden/enclosure as the capture of an (Eden) that is complete in one sense (since the parenthesis does enclose meaning), yet ineffective in another sense, as it is visibly broken.

This casts light on *Vierzehnheiligen*, I think. The oval & the repetition of the oval, represents a different stylistic description of the process.

While I am talking about concrete poetry, can I mention that the TLS, in a survey taken in a random set of libraries, has discovered my anthology to be well up among the most frequently held post-war poetry books?! Before Peter Porter (tho' after the Liverpool scene).

What you say about the Museum of Modern Art fills me with foreboding. Wasn't there some distant spectre called Fernbach-Flarsheim (how unlikely it seems!)? No doubt he is in charge & will fill the Museum with wailing and gnashing of type.

Stupidly I have mislaid the *Ships Monthly* address. I enclose a letter & wonder if this is suitable to be sent on to the Editor?

I have now written to Karpel pointing out that he owes you both an acknowledgment of the poems (provided they are there) & a reimbursement for crating & postage. I hope he will respond soon. But frankly the more I try to communicate with America, the less I subscribe to the myth of their super-efficiency.

I do apologise for baulking at the task of approaching the French magazine. The point is that I showed the photos to [Bernard] Lassus & he definitely thought they would be incomprehensible to French editors without quite detailed explanation (in French of course). I couldn't frankly say that I would have the time to work on this until early August. But at that stage I might be able to do something in collaboration with Frank Popper. Is that alright? I think it is certainly the best chance as far as *L'Oeil* goes. But if, say, an English magazine wanted the photos, it might be best to send them there.

I look forward to Christopher Carrell's news & send all best wishes to Sue, Eck & Ailie,

love from

Stephen

Stonypath
22 June 1971

Dear Stephen,

thank you so much for your nice letter, which I was delighted to get.

"The Voice of the sea-trout is heard in the Land" – is a most memorable sentence.[31] My Domestic Pensées wee book is quite envious of it. (I must show you this Random Notebook of Unruled Lines, when you next visit Stonypath.)[32]

I am hastening to reply to your letter as Michael Harvey arrives tomorrow, for the great Stonypath Sundial Week – what a shame we missed The Longest Day. This will certainly be my greatest experiment in construction, employing not only a 'real' sculptor but a 'real' builder's labourer, to mix the tons of cement, far up the hill . . .

Thank you for the book of poems.[33] I am not as against the mode as you might think. I will read the book carefully, at supper-times, (that interlude which we have before going to bed), and I will make sensible (I hope) comments in due course. I like the dignified appearance: it is a very proper 'first poems' sort of format.

Thank you, Stephen.

I am fascinated by your Garden as Parenthesis[34] because I have already used the same figure as

(the) (footprints) (of) (the) barge)

– not arranged quite like that, and I think I perhaps said footsteps rather than prints. In fact, this poem – which was published in 1963 (?) in a limited edition of 7 copies, is going to reappear in "A Jiffy Bag", a new and uncollected collection, not yet quite ready for Michael Harvey's lettering . . .

31. My reference to seasonal produce is based on a verse from the Song of Solomon (King James version): 'The voice of the turtle [i.e. turtle-dove] is heard in our land.'

32. Finlay's *Domestic Pensées (1964–1972)* were published by Stuart Mills in Aggie Weston's editions (2004).

33. Anthony Grist, *Causes: Poems 1968–70* (W. E. Baxter Ltd, 1971)

34. This poem (referring to the gardening ideas of William Morris) would be published as a card by Tarasque Press later in the year.

> pl. 19

One day we ought to do a Garden Book together.

I have been speculating – from the more practical aspect – in the idea of the garden as an enclosed thing. For a while (in my inexperience) I was greatly perplexed as to why Stonypath did not have a garden-y garden; and I eventually realised that it was the lack of enclosing verticals – a situation we are slowly remedying – lack of cash preventing a fell-swoop-solution, (which is perhaps no bad thing). The trellis-work for the roses, was a first step. Now I have reached the last (or wood-carver) stage with a new sundial, as a post, which is to re-introduce the rose-trellis vertical, half-way down the garden.[35] These things are variations on your theme.

The news that your anthology is "well up among the most frequently held post-war poetry books", (re the TLS), is absolutely splendid. It represents one of those triumphs of the obvious (which one saw) over Improbability (which everyone else saw, not least – I dare say – Mr J. Willett.) I am delighted. The book deserves it: but what a book deserves it does not (alas) always get. Good for you. Hurray.

Fernbach-Flarsheim:[36] in the wet bracken he discovers the silvery hues of an old thermos-flask interior, glinting, and smelling a little (still) of the fumes of Flars, (a frightful Nordic drink). On the interior is the legend: Made in Wales.

This is a piece of what is called free-association.

Please forgive it.

(Bach, old pal.)

I have sent on your letter to Ships Monthly. This was a jolly good letter – just right. Then, that is super (may I continue on this paper, instead of rising from the floor to rummage in THE WILD HAWTHORN PRESS), that you have written Mr Carp-el – El Karp, the Oldest Spanish Denizen of The Pool – ; and we will see what aspect of the epic comes next . . . As for the

35. The vertical wooden sundial, carved by John R. Thorpe (and with a red gnomon) formed a prominent feature of the garden when my film, *Stonypath Days*, was shot in July 1973. It was illustrated in 'Selected Ponds' (*West Coast Poetry Review*, 1975) under the title 'Sundial FR 64, Fr 195'. As a wooden structure, it finally decayed and was removed from the garden, but it is due to be reconstructed and reinstalled in 2016.

36. See my reference in the previous letter. In 1970 the German artist Carl Fernbach-Flarsheim had devised a programme called Conceptual Typewriter to generate spatial outputs of letters.

French magazine, if you really might be able to tackle the thing, with Frank Popper, in August, that would be grand. My wish is that we should not abandon the project altogether, and I fully understand that there have been other things to do, (to put it mildly).

Christopher Carrell assures me that he is 'writing' to you – am ambiguous tense, at best. But he is an amiable chap.

I had a further letter from Mary Ellen, about MOMA (dear Lord) and the Great Exhibition. Apparently The Designing Designers, having told her false stories over a New York Lunch, have circulated a lot of poets, asking them to ignore the proposed exhibition. This was splendid news, and I have a wee hope that the Designing Designers might circulate ALL the poets, save us. Dear Mary Ellen, she is a sweet good soul.

Did I tell you I have (meanwhile) fallen in love with battleships? I was converted quite suddenly, (as soon as the battleship entered the room and stood looking around, ill-at-ease, and uncertain where to put down its drink). These delightful creations, says Robert One-K-Kenedy, are wicked. In fact, unlike other forms of wickedness which I might mention (said he darkly), they are all dead (for a kick-off). And again, there is the way they combine an image of Necessity, with one of Miracle (which sank Necessity), as well as Belligerence with Vulnerability – spelling? – and Grace. I will show you battleship photos when you come. Meanwhile (on the principle that one must walk before one can run) I am building a model frigate. It is rather nice. I have also ordered a copy of a publication named Battleship International: I believe it is not edited by Commander Robert Tait.[37]

I will shortly be sending you my Frightful Holiday Postcard.[38] Will you be at Canterbury?

It was super to have your letter. Love,

Ian

37. The Scottish poet (and editor of the magazine *Scottish International*), Robert Tait figures frequently in the letters published in *Midway* (see pp. 354–64).

38. *Homage to Donald McGill* (see p. 120).

Canterbury
15 July [1971]

Dear Ian,

It was splendid to receive your letter & to get the naughty sea-side postcard in the interval. Now that my mind is set on beaches & bathing costumes shortly to be donned, the suggestion is all the more seasonal. I set off for Jersey on Monday & shall be spending a week there beside the old fishing port of St Aubin. Besides general living apparatus I shall be taking Pater's *Imaginary Portraits*, in a slim edition, & M. Butor's recent variations on a theme of Diabelli by Beethoven.[39] From Jersey (where the Hawkinses – Oliver, Diana & my goddaughter Olivia take their leave) I shall be touring Brittany with a friend who has concealed about him *Weir of Hermiston*.[40] Eventually I shall be in the Pyrenees, scene of an improbable **FESTIVAL OF LIGHT & MOVEMENT**, at which I shall meet the Poppers & put finishing touches to a work on Agam.

This expansive prospect quite put me in mind of all I have to complete before launching off into the Azure. I have spent much of the past week or two attending to translations of two unusual pieces entitled 'Soft Architecture' and 'Plasters on a wooden leg'; also writing a nasty review of various books on Paolozzi & others, in which I manage to say nice things about Albers (bless his furry tale) for the TLS, also completing my interminable study of Thackeray's *Henry Esmond* with a brief end-piece in which it is shown that (structurally) *H.E.* is *Quentin Durward* backwards.[41]

But I have had the opportunity to reply to Chris Carrell's request for a synopsis of my proposed essay. I have sent it off, & he will be able no doubt to include it in his submission. I have also heard from **KARPEL**, who writes in a rather elliptical way as if he were dictating from the shower. He is apparently sending the money for postage & some purchases, but was surprised at the cost of posting & number of works (which, as he said – send everything – is a bit odd). Anyhow he admires your 'craftsmanship'.

39. Michel Butor, *Dialogue avec 33 variations de Ludwig van Beethoven sur une valse de Diabelli* (Gallimard, 1971).

40. Robert Louis Stevenson's 'unfinished romance', published posthumously in 1896.

41. In my review article for *TLS* 3622 (30 July 1971), I criticised a study of the Scottish sculptor Eduardo Paolozzi, while praising Werner Spies's short book on Josef Albers. Around this time, the Finlays' cat was named after the noted Bauhaus and Black Mountain College artist Albers. My article on *Henry Esmond* would be published in the French journal, *Poétique*, in 1972.

I wonder how the great Sundial week went off. It should be most exciting. And I must make a tentative enquiry about the mechanics of the thing in view of the possibility of having one here at Kent, on our windswept hillside. The point is that, having been elevated to the office of Chairman of the Senate Exhibitions Committee, I am in the position of having certain funds at my disposal (provided my committee is amenable). The architect stands like Cerberus in defence of the university site, but even he can be suborned no doubt.

Anyhow it is a possible chink in the future. I have delicately raised the subject with several people & all are favourable. But maybe another stone poem would be easier than a sundial. It would be interesting to know what you felt appropriate –

I hope, by the way, to be able to come to Stonypath in late August, if that is a convenient time. It would be not the sort of sandwiched visit that I seem to make most times. That is to say, it would of course be sandwiched between other episodes – but the bread would be more yielding.

I must break off at this point & wish you a pleasant summery few weeks – in case I do not hear from you in France (though I shall certainly send a postcard or two). For the next week I shall be highly accessible c/o Mrs Pilkington, La Vielle Maison, The Bulwarks, St Aubin, Jersey (leaving 26 July) but after that it is more uncertain. The best bet (3–10 August) is Poste Restante, LUCHON, Haute-Garonne, France.

Love to Sue, Eck &Ailie,
Yours

Stephen

PS I'm so glad the garden poem interests you. Now I seem to need only one more card to complete the sequence.[42]

40. The sequence would be completed by 'Doves over the Sarthe at Solesmes', which was published as a poem card by Tarasque Press towards the end of the year.

Stonypath
20 July 1971

Dear Old Stephen,

it was super to have your letter and to know that you are still there somewhere, there or there, or there, as the case may be. I am glad that the Blue Postcard reached you, and I wonder if the little folded card got to Canterbury before you left? I thought it might just . . possibly . .

Are you taking Imaginary Portraits to St Aubin on my recommendation – or did I forget to urge you to read this most delightful of books . .? It is my Favourite Book of All. Moreover, I think you might well write a kind of contemporary sequel: do not treat this suggestion as frivolous.[43]

Weir of Hermiston

(water weir

water

wee-er water)

reminds me that All Is Changed, Utterly Changed, since I last wrote, for, in addition to Le Grand Sundial Week, we have had an Interlude of Bulldozers and the Loch is now complete but for the water, a state of affairs which is rather more dramatic than it sounds. The bulldozers themselves would delight any latterday Marinetti, though the drivers were very nice, and one of them, leaning down from the cab of his fifteen-ton machine, asked me whether there were any particular bits of the landscape which I wished to be 'titivated' (sic). (The expression titivated by a bulldozer has passed into my repertoire.) But, these have been hectic days, and we are still toiling to complete the water's exits before it reaches the (height of the) sluice – which I hope is large enough to take all Highland Spates . . Bricoleur, dear Stephen, is the word for it – as you will see when, in late August, you stand atop the formidable earthworks, looking down on the ant-like Eck (or the Eck-like ants) far below. I am aghast at what I have taken on; let us only hope it holds.

43. The book had indeed been strongly recommended to me by Finlay (see p. 99). In 1977, my most substantial commentary on Finlay's work to date (the opening essay for the catalogue of his Arts Council show at the Serpentine Gallery) would be entitled: 'Ian Hamilton Finlay: An Imaginary Portrait'.

Sundial Week (which seems like Remote History) was not a success. Michael is an excellent companion, and we had a good time; but the actual moulds proved too weak, as I foresaw (from my experience of casting pavingstones), with the result that the concrete caused sagging, which turned the bevel (intended to facilitate release), into a lock. One sundial is ruined and will have to be recast, (something that should prove very possible now that Michael has a clearer idea of the weight of the stuff); the other sundial may be all right; I have to make a decision after trying some patching, and this has been delayed by the pressure (as it were) of water (gathering in its Loch below).

I would be delighted to have a sundial at Canterbury. Let us do our uttermost to realise the project (which can be discussed when you come). My feeling about concrete now is, that it is a good medium, but is really only a sensible choice if one is going to cast 6 off, rather than 1, for the cost of the preparation of the mould is such, that it is really cheaper to do a single work – even a large-scale one – in stone. The Biggar Sundial shows how very effective the large-scale in stone can be. If, however, I ever had a market for my things (a very remote eventuality) I would not hesitate to use concrete, preparing a mould with a professional firm (to which Michael could supply detailed drawings).

Meanwhile, the garden has grown a nice new oak poem-bench[44] and a delightful rendering in stone of 'Bring Back The Birch', which fronts the little grove of Wild Cherries near the large Ash. This little poem is a triumph, for it shows a great advance in the garden, that it has taken a Roman-roofed little Inscription into one of its groves.

Meanwhile, at the back, we are faced with acres of red earthworks, to be planted with grass seed, as well as a tangled network of waterways which render Stonypath The Venice of The North.

I was so encouraged (and pleased) to hear that you have arranged the catalogue/monograph with Christopher Carrell. That is really something to look forward to. I imagine that one part of your thesis will be illustrated (illumined by) a poem/print now in preparation, a splendid and audacious sequel to 'Homage to Mozart', the beautiful World War II warship Prinz Eugen, subtitled (in appropriate l[ower]c[ase] Helvetica), 'homage to gomringer'.

44. This is presumably the tripartite 'Tree-Bench', carved by Vincent Butler, which was placed around the large ash tree at the end of the Front Garden, close to the grove containing 'Bring Back The Birch'.

> pl. 5

This broadside – as well as honouring an earlier era – opens the great Battleship Epoch (which supersedes fishingboats).

This reminds me – why? – that we had a making-it-up visit from Big Jonathan Williams, followed by a Very Surprise visit from wee Ernst Jandl, together with – of all people – Yeddie [Morgan], and an Intrepid Arts Council Official from London, Charles Osborne.[45] We sat upon the new terrace (sic). 'You will have to excuse the steady roar of my bulldozers', I said, or words to that effective effect.

Ernst was looking very round and well, and Big J was looking very round and not so well, and indeed rather sad; I am glad to be pals again.

My next task, apart from completing my model frigate, is to build a Mooring Buoy for the larger dinghy, which is to sit in the middle of the Loch, with waves lapping at its bows.

The response from KARPEL is very depressing. It could scarcely have been worse. To have one's 'craftsmanship' admired, is a bit like having one's 'integrity' admired: it means the other person has happened briefly and will scarcely be seen in the vicinity again.

May I gently remind you about Mr Popper, and L'oeil and the photos of my garden-poems and the projected article . . . (said he guiltily). I take it Ships Monthly has not yet replied to your excellent letter?

My other little German book, The Olsen Excerpts,[46] is to be ready this evening, in Gottingen, the publisher phoned to assure me; it has been very quick. The other other German book is at present the subject of discussion, which threatens to become debate.

Our garbage-heap, behind the byre, is now largely covered with earth and looks but a Pale ozzi. This reminds me that I have hit upon the happy and dismissive idea, of always picturing Edward Wright in a kilt. Now you will, too.

Happy Voyagings, keep well, love from all, Your Appreciative Pal,

Ian

45. Charles Osborne occupied the post of Literature Director of the Arts Council of Great Britain from 1971 to 1986.

46. *The Olsen Excerpts*, with photographs by Diane Tammes, Verlag Udo Breger, Göttingen, 1971. The fishing boat lists that alternate with Diane Tammes's photographs are reprinted directly from Olsen's *Fisherman's Nautical Almanac*.

Write when you can.

PS 'Tri-Quarterly 21', an American Magazine, has arrived, as a prelude to the Swallow Press publication 'Contemporary British Poetry'. There is a large-ish colour section on my stuff, with a stunning colour photo of the **KY** – wish we could borrow the blocks for the monograph . . . (Will show you in August)

Stonypath
27 July 1971

Dear Stephen,

I have no idea whether your letters are being forwarded to you on your holiday(s). A wish to have done with distasteful subjects, prompts me to forward this copy to Canterbury – that I may the more quickly forget all about it, (having reduced the original recipient to a thoughtful and far-away silence, I hope).[47] I think the letter explains the (long-standing) circumstance. I really do get very tired of Modern Youth.

Strange as it must seem to you, we are all still here, at Stonypath – nowadays with a new loch upon our (so to speak) hands. We are busy sewing seed and digging new ditches. My first little neon poem is to arrive tomorrow afternoon.

My affection for battleships increases.

'The Olsen Excerpts', my new little book published in Gottingen, arrived today, and is very nice, I think. The publisher sent a copy Express (which seems extraordinary) and put in a wee note saying that he thought it his nicest publication to date (which seemed almost too good to be true.)

All for now, as I sit here nursing my outworn elbow at The Sign of The Nudge (see letter to SC.). How is the Festival of Light? Love,

Ian

47. The copy letter of 27 July that Finlay enclosed was addressed to Simon Cutts, and quoted back Cutts's observation that Finlay's 'system' was 'wearing at the elbow'. Comments on this exchange are included in my return letter, and in Finlay's response to me of 18 August. According to a letter sent to me on 7 September by Cutts, the disagreements had begun with their joint publication of *Allotments* in December 1970. He predicted that the dispute would soon be over, which proved to be the case.

Canterbury
14 August [19]71

Dear Ian,

I have so many things to thank you for – to begin with the two letters, one received in Jersey & the other on my return home the day before yesterday. And then, the various poems, the last of which popped through the letter-box & wedged itself into the draught-excluder (quite retrievably) yesterday morning. To start with 'Old Nobby', I am much pleased with the conjunction of 'old' text and old (tinted) photograph. We are still only on the point of recognising what atmosphere the photograph clusters to itself (a recent exhibition of that splendid Scottish photographer Hill/Adamson seemed to reveal 19thc. Rembrandts by the series – & doesn't the example of the inspired Mrs Cameron suggest a significant proportion of excellent early photographers to have been Scottish?). *Tree-shells* is a fine piece also, but I suppose I am particularly taken by *Evening/Sail* 2, which is somehow intimately what I am inclined to or interested in.[48] Perhaps not since the end of *Ocean Stripe* 5 have I felt that particular strong impression (of form/atmosphere) so keenly.

My recent holidays have been a model of tripartite arrangement. First of all, sand-castles & lobsters & sand-between-the-toes & all that kind of thing on various Jersey locations – Olivia, my god-daughter of less than 1, superintended by parents, managed to look quite primally pink against the beach-scape. We dined off snipe, the local fish/metaphor as follows:

It has to be cut enough to go into the frying pan & discloses bright green bones beneath its appetising flesh. I assure you I didn't dream it!

Then there was a week of hard but rewarding trudging in Brittany & thereabouts with Tony Grist. It gave rise to a sort of poetic journal in which I found myself (a little unexpectedly) placing Kiplingesque verses. I must send you my 'Hymn to Saint Philibert' which begins with the refrain:

48. This notable screen-print, which was reedited in 1991 by the Graeme Murray Gallery, is sometimes dated 1970, but appears in fact to have been published in 1971. The same text, in a different format, was used for the 'Evening/Sail' sundial, carved by John R. Thorpe, which is shown installed beside the Middle Pond in my colour photograph dated September 1971 (see p. 105). The title 'Evening/Sail 2' indicates the relationship to the prior sundial text.

> pl. 7

The fury of the Northmen
Hath driven us away
The ravage of the long ships
Laid waste Noirmoutier
The body of Saint Philibert
We bear upon our way.

& continues (why not indeed?):

We passed the Breton marshes,
We crossed the Loire in spate,
And so we came to Grand-Lieu
Before the Abbey gate.
We eased our precious burden
And scarce had breath to say:
The fury of the Northmen
Hath driven us away.

The Abbot raised our burden
His gain supplied our loss.
He cased it in blue marble
Sealed with an ancient cross.
We ate & drank & worshipped
And soon forgot the day:
The fury of the Northmen
Laid waste Noirmoutier.

Years passed. Again the Northmen
Began to range afar.
They passed the Breton marshes,
They crossed the brimming Loire.
And we were old & weary
But we could never stay.
The body of Saint Philibert
We bore upon our way.

We kept the Loire to northwards,
Our strength was not our own.
It was the saint who led us
To Tournus on the Saône.
All honour to Saint Philibert!
We will forget the day

The ravage of the long ships
Laid waste Noirmoutier.
The body of Saint Philibert
Is laid to rest for ay.

It is, as you might expect, a true story.

The final element of my holiday was a little more than a week at Néris-les-Bains, a French spa specialising in rheumatism, where Frank Popper & I managed, by a process of intensive collaboration, to end up with a fairly substantial monograph on Agam, one of the more enigmatic & interesting kinetic artists.[49] Aline Popper has undertaken to revise & put in final French form anything I may do for *L'Oeil*. So I can start getting that into order.

It really now seems only a week or two before I shall be able to come up to Scotland & see you all. Will the last weekend in August – i.e. c. 27 August – be an acceptable time? It will be splendid to see all the new installations, with the bulldozers buzzing like somnolent hornets (or have they finally migrated for the autumn?). Do you remember suggesting that it might be possible to arrange a showing of our graveyard film, *Never-standing Time*, together with one of yours? I wonder if that is still conceivable.

And this reminds me of a request I promised to put to you. The film's co-author, Tony Grist, is really very anxious to meet you & see Stonypath. If I came up for 2 or 3 days, would there be room/willingness for him to arrive on the last day & then travel back with me? He is not at all a typical example of modern youth, being in general extremely shy & serious (& likely to end up in the Anglican church with a graveyard of his own).[50] Of course, if this time were not convenient, we could always make it another. He was, incidentally, most overwhelmed by your Vuillard interior[51] & asked me to get one from you – perhaps that could be sent (with bill, of course) in the mean time?

At this point, it is perhaps appropriate to say how shocked I was by the phrases from Simon that you quote in your letter. Is it perhaps that he doesn't realise

49. This was a change from our original plan of meeting at Luchon in the Pyrenees. Popper's study of Agam was finally published in 1976, and several expanded editions were to follow.

50. Anthony Grist subsequently became Rector of St Elisabeth's Church, Reddish, near Stockport in Lancashire, but resigned the post in 1986. In 1973, his parents commissioned the first of Finlay's sundials to be installed in a private garden for their house near Tonbridge in East Kent. This was carved by Michael Harvey.

51. *Homage to Vuillard* (with Michael Harvey) evokes a domestic interior by the French painter, Édouard Vuillard (1868–1940).

(through the swathes of Mallarmé-an prose) how wounding & unjust his remarks are? It is really very puzzling, as well as saddening. I suppose one can see it as a kind of subconscious rejection of an influence he feels too dominant in his own work.

To more pleasant subjects – Walter Pater's *Imaginary Portraits* were taken on holiday entirely on your recommendation, & they are absolutely exquisite. I read them just in the last few days of my holiday & the pathos of *Denys l'Auxerrois*, just as I was leaving the Loire behind, quite overcame me. I have now bought & am reading *Miscellaneous Studies*. It may have some equally good essays in it. The first one I looked at – 'Emerald Uthwatt' – at least contains a marvellous epitome of England: 'our land of vignettes'. How about that as the title of a garden book? That, incidentally, is already taking form in my mind. I can see us 'borrowing' people's gardens, & putting (as with National Trust, & 'Gardens open to the public'): 'By kind permission of . . . . .'

I had better close now, hoping that all is well at Stonypath & looking forward to see[ing] you soon –

yours

Stephen

Stonypath
18 August 1971

Dear Stephen,

it was lovely to hear from you! How The Summer has wheeched away . . . I was delighted to have all your news.

First, we will look forward very much to seeing you on 27 August, to be joined by Tony Grist on the third day. (Or Last Day, as the case may be.) We would gladly invite Tony Grist for all the days, but it <u>is</u> a fact that two guests are almost too much for our wee house and large children. I am very serious in my hope that we will be able to add a floating bedroom, or little loch-yacht, for next year: so that you and Tony may come for longer and be properly housed (or cabined) – will you explain this to Tony? Meanwhile we will be <u>delighted</u> to welcome you both, in stages, in the way you suggest in your letter.

I cannot remember when I last wrote to you, (a circumstance arising from the fact that I had no clear idea of when you might get my letter). Anyway, we are all here.

The Parliamentary Commissioner has at last Reported, and his Conclusion is, as Judith Hart observed, 'a total confirmation' of my assertion that the Fulcrum edition is not a first. On the other hand, the PC fails to relate this Conclusion to the behaviour of Lord Eccles, and is not allowed, in terms of his Office, to relate it to that of Lord Goodman. I need not say that I will be pleased to do this myself, as soon as I have a spare moment. Judith Hart has written to say that she means to ask for an Adjournment Debate in The House, in October: I will have to make sure that Rubinstein/Fulcrum hear of this in advance.

Did I also tell you that the Large Sundials are melancholy ruins, awaiting removal? A Disaster, but an entirely redeemable one. In the case of 'Land/Sea' I am sure that a casting by a professional firm, off-site, would be a total success, and I hope you may feel that this would be a suitable project for Canterbury. Meanwhile, Michael Harvey is going to cut me a smaller (identical) version on a rock (which I am obtaining from the seashore), and I will perhaps attempt the large version again next year – it is really a super sundial.[52]

The grass is growing up, around the new loch.

I am working at Pond 4 – or is it 5?

As for the Simon question, your kind words are much appreciated. I am less hurt than exasperated, in that there are few people with whom one can discuss Poetry and Simon ought to be one of them. My 'Flags' postcard was intended as a friendly celebration of a particular affinity, yet it did not get so much as a bare acknowledgment from Simon . . while he observed of the 'Sea Street' postcard that he does not like names in the street. This was the last straw. Now that I expect nothing in the way of response I feel neither angry nor hurt. And I cannot think of any contemporary poet I enjoy reading more. (Though I would welcome the news that Tarasque has severed its relations with the horrendous Miss Print.)

Stuart [Mills] was here for a pleasant weekend.

52. For this version of 'Land/Sea' on a stone from the seashore, see *Ian Hamilton Finlay: An Illustrated Essay*, pl. 37. Finlay's plan for a 'large version' would be fulfilled in the Canterbury Sundial.

I greatly enjoyed your Kiplingesque poem, though it must be said that it is less K. than my Medieval Latin Lyric Penguin. I also have a little poem about (as Simon would say) long ships; you will see it Anon. Your poem reminds me to ask if you know The Oxford Book of Irish Verse: I am sure you would rejoice in the early poems of Austin ('Honey By The Water') Clarke . . and I will list others for you, if you have the book to hand . . .

Our Visiting Season has been very slow in starting, but we are now awaiting a photographer, and a large truck which is to empty our Cesspool, and the Television People who are to come and film me in conversation with Richard Demarco . . . (a frightful prospect). We have also just had one of those letters which begin: "Helloa Ian" and ebb, I meant to say end, with a name one has never heard, in between proposing A Visit which it is too late to postpone (since it is timed to start the next day). "This is Richard . . This is, I-forget-your-name . . This is the Tellyman . .. This is the man who is driving the truck which is going to empty our Cesspool . . . This is the photographer . . This is Sue's Mother . . . And this is a Surprise Visitor . . Who can it be? (It is like the one who came on Sunday, disguised as John Lennon, and who took off a bit of a garden-sundial and wore it as a ring . .)

I enclose a Wee Present from Gottingen.[53] We look forward to seeing you and are sending the Vuillard separately but without delay. It was super to have your Summer Letter. Aye,

Ian

Canterbury
11 September [1971]

Dear Ian,

It is just about exactly a week since we arrived at Stonypath, just in time for the illusory Private View & the Rumanian artists' Regatta (amateur class).[54] It was a really splendid stay & I shall add it to the souvenir of my last visit in representing the capacity of Dunsyre to attain unexpected heights of

53. *The Olsen Excerpts* (see note 42).

54. The visit had begun with my remarking that the press of cars outside the farm gate at Stonypath seemed to augur a Private View (a misconception that greatly amused the Finlays). The visiting artists from Romania, brought *en masse* to Stonypath by Richard Demarco, and venturing to set sail on the lochan, confirmed our suspicion that theirs was not a sea-going nation.

weather. Tony encloses a letter of thanks, & I know he was quite enchanted by the whole visit.

The time elapsing between then & now has been sufficient for a network of communication to be established between Stonypath, Bridport & Canterbury. Michael Harvey (whose exquisite script should have been immediately recognisable from the envelope) proposes coming to visit the University towards the end of October. That will be excellent. I must try and ensure that the University architect is softened up in the mean time (by the insidious device of approaching him through his daughters).[55] Michael Harvey has offered to send large pictures of 'Land/Sea' & I shall be able to show them to my committee.

The small *Land/Sea* is now installed, at a rakish (or alternatively Suprematist) angle by one of my windows. I have arranged it so that it reads from behind, so to speak (since the other side of the house is rather in the shade). It tells the afternoon time very successfully & is altogether a fine addition to the room. I must really start thinking about the possibility of an outdoor sundial, as the garden (front or back) would effectively accommodate one. I chanced to see one in a local antique shop, but the detailing was oddly crude & the inscription, in so far as it was legible, read 'HOURS BE SWEET * 1932': not the right cultural aura, perhaps . . .

I shall be setting off for Stockholm next weekend. I wonder if it will be possible to take the Stonypath prospectus? If you have available copies by mid-week, do send a few. I am a bit sceptical of entering the lair of Dr Pontus Hulten, & taking part in the participatory experience of his porno-kinetic paradise (if that is the right description). But I can always take refuge with my two Swedish friends, both of whom happen to be very religious (maybe Sweden affects them like that); one is a cross between a Plymouth Brother and a Catholic & the other more conventionally Protestant.

I have started to think in more concrete terms (as appropriate to a solid work) of my Ceolfrith essay/monograph. It will have four discrete sections, one of them polemical, another lyrical, a third art-historical & a fourth in a vein not yet established. I look forward to writing it, & shall be glad to get the printing schedule & format settled before too long.

55. I had met the University Architect, Bill Henderson, a few years before, while on holiday in Scotland, and became a friend of his eldest daughter, Tessa.

I rather think the time has come to remove an enormous cake from the oven. It comes from an Edwardian collection of recipes & might be indicated for 'when the Vicar makes his five o'clock call'. Perplexingly enough, it contains **SAL VOLATILE**, though not in sufficient quantities to cure anybody's vapours. Today is a highly experimental day in the kitchen: by 10 o'clock I shall have been whisked away in a 'Pumpkin au gratin'.

Thank you once again, Ian. It was a super weekend & I look forward to the next.

Yours

Stephen

Stonypath
17 September [19]71

Dear Stephen,

I am writing to you just as you are about to set off for Sweden, which is not very sensible of me (and very daring of you). No matter; it was lovely to have the letters from you and Tony, and I am most pleased that you enjoyed your wee visit. Tony is so nice that even I – optimist as I am – would scarcely have thought he could actually exist. It was a great pleasure to have you both, and it is very nice, and refreshing to have such friends.

As a matter of fact, and on reflection (during a long pause denoted by the little space above this sentence), I think that you and Tony should be toured by the Arts Council as an Example and Event. (By an imaginary, superior Arts Council, I mean.) I would be delighted to write an appreciative Introduction.

We have had many visitors since you were here. I have rather lost count of them all. Derek [Stanford]'s wife – as if anticipating the arrival of *Tristram's Sail*, (my new sundial-poem, now in the pond immediately behind the house) – sailed in a very upright fated sort of way, and sure enough, it was not very long before her sail (Peggy's) was in the loch too. Sue helped her out. The neo-Romanian Hellenestic [sic] trousers had to be fetched from the drawer once again . . . More recently we were visited by a lady from New York, who was sent by the chap who did the typography for the large Calendar; I suppose she was more a girl than a lady; she was really very nice, and laughed a great deal, and told me all about the mysteries of macro(?)biotic food, (which are a matter of Yin and Yang, that knockabout pair of whom one has heard . .)

I now have a clear, if not wholly accurate, picture of Microbiotic Restaurants – people sitting on the floor eating raisins off last week's New York Times.

I had an agonised, heavy-breathing 'phonecall from Ian Gardner, who had just resigned from Tarasque. He explained that his resigning would not make any difference, but that his telling me would make his resignation real, or more real, than his merely telling Stuart (who, by Ian's account, merely looked at him silently 'and went to bed', I quote.)

Our Wild Hawthorn Lists have arrived this very day, just too late for you to take to Sweden.

I am very excited to hear about the monograph. If you would like to write to the fabled Mr Hummerstone of Stellar Press, here is the address: Welham Green, Hatfield, Herts. Mr Hummerstone will help you with advice about size and page-numbers, I am sure.

During Michael's visit (which only ended yesterday) we discussed the sundial, and we decided that we must not be limited to a consideration of the concrete 'Land/Sea', in that the site might demand something a little different. I reminded Michael that the Biggar Sundial shows how well these pre-Socratic anticipations of The Future, (and hopefully, of the Present, or at least The Solar Present), translate into dark slate. The whole matter can be discussed by us all, with reference to the site and everything else; it is a most encouraging possibility.

> pls. 14, 15

I do wish you had seen Tristram's Sail, but of course you will see it next year. It took to my pond immediately.

As I think I intimated, we are having a whopping Financial Crisis (perhaps as a consequence of Floating our Sundials)* [*instead of our Yens] so that it seems hopelessly optimistic to think of sending anything to a printer ever again. However, on the basis that one should anticipate the possibility of success, do you think it would be possible to fit your monograph-plans in, with a wee half-plan of mine, which is this:

To produce, before December, a properly printed but brief little publication on my neon-poems. The purpose of this would be, to explain the meaning of the poems to any visitors (and critics) at the Richard Demarco Gallery (Richard Demarco Street, Richard Demarco), as they will otherwise not understand them (just as they do not understand my unlit poems). The format would be modest, and essentially the thing would consist of some photos of the works, and a bit of text, amounting to (say) about 1000 words, or 2000, or somewhere between.

My idea is, that if these words were yours, they might actually be written as a section of the proposed book, so that, if I failed to find the cash (or cool nerve) to produce the pamphlet (ah, that is the word I have been seeking) for the exhibition, still, the whole text could be used – would in any case be used – in your book. Do you think this would be possible, Stephen?

There is the obvious disadvantage that you have not seen the other works, and I am hoping that you could reconstruct them from your memory of 'barque'. In case this is so, I will list them here, with comments.

barque is a little like starting a new medium by returning to the 'classical' stage of Concrete Poetry, instanced by Gomringer's wind (etc.), the white (neon) light establishing a 'concrete' image (of the sails of the barque) in a 'pure concrete' manner. And as concrete poetry has allowed a sort of revival of the inscription, (the old revitalised in the perspective of the new), so in this case, pure concrete poetry (which it is somehow very hard to write now) becomes possible again by the addition of the element of light; one is not simply repeating oneself but repeating the possibility of pure concrete simplicity. (All badly expressed but you see my point).

blue water's bark will be realised in blue light, in a handwritten style. 'blue water' is a kind of sailor's synonym (spelling?) for deep water, or ocean-voyaging. The word 'bark' does service as both sailing-ship (barque being sometimes spelt in that way) and as the tree-stuff which parallels the texture of rippled water. This is that kind of 'self-sufficient fragment', or pure sensation (or perception) stabilised, which I find so entrancing.

wave is a white light (neon) version of the 'wave' poem on 2 pages of the Macmillan book, the one which manages to turn the typist's (or proof reader's) ∽ sign, into a pre-Socratic reference. You will be familiar with the little (tiny) kinetic booklet version of this work, which the neon version presents in a single line of repeated waves and ∽ signs. (Or wa∽evs and signs, etc.)

Sails/Waves is also all in white, and is simply a neon version of the postcard I did with Ron Costley.[56] The conventional doodle 〰 which means waves or clouds or whatever, is punned upon (as it were) by standing one

56. *Sails/Waves* 1, design for a wall ceramic.

series of doodle-curves upright, and labelling them 'sails'. The arrow-shapes (if you will consult the postcard) make a clear reference to those arrow-shapes which haunt the Greek alphabet . . and the whole is of the pre-Socratic universe-naming thing-and-order-enjoying sort. But you will note that the shorthand doodle for the sails, represents not a Greek boat, but a brig, brigantine, or some European (at any rate) sophisticated square-rigged boat (see for example "homage to 'Mozart'") which is a nice, and witty, appreciation of our culture, a little like the 'Azure and Son' of the Biggar sundial (if you see what I mean).

And that is all . . though if I can find the cash I will do, next, the fleet of peaches in neon, using the 'translation' and the French, alternately (as I am assured can be very easily done by means of a little motor. I feel – perhaps over hopefully – that some explanation along these lines (more or less) might add the dawning (neon) light of recognition to certain eyes . . and if I cannot do the pamphlet, the whole might well fit into the monograph, for the idea of the neon barque as a kind of renewal of pure concrete – that glorious experience of our golden youth! – pleases me mightily, and seems Stephen-esque in its potentialities of instancing a number of relevant thoughts . . .

And here I will stop. I have one of those nagging little colds which come to nothing but which yet contrive to blot all, a kind of Zurbrugg (as it were) of a cold (rather than a forthright and aspirinable Henri Chopin.)

It was grand to see you, and to meet Tony, who is very nice, and much appreciated (for neither of you are the Out of Sight, Out of Mind sort of friends, who leave one downcast and willingly forgetful.)

Love,

aye,

Ian

Stonypath
24 September [19]71

Dear Stephen,

I am not sure how long you were staying in Sweden. I suppose the Swedes manage to stay there for quite long stretches, but it seems likely that you would be there only for the proverbial wee while. Anyway, this is an extra letter, which can await your return.

I want to raise a specific point which has rendered the morning unhappy, and which may cloud the evening less if I can discuss it with you (knowing you for a civilised pal). It concerns a bill I have just had from Michael Harvey, in respect of the 'wild' stone version of 'Land/Sea', which he recently came up to cut. I am shattered to discover that the bill includes £24 for travelling time, and £10 for petrol. I am shattered because the stone was cut, in the first place, to resolve the summer debacle with the cast concrete sundials, and then I am also shattered because Michael's visit was virtually a three-day holiday for him: he spent a great deal of time sailing (Use of boat, £15-15), and was nobly looked after by Sue (Food, Bed, and Extras, £35).

To revert to the sundials, I am (as I have said) delighted with these as projects, and the disaster lay entirely in the casting and the construction of the moulds. It is sad to have to recount that Michael originally took no responsibility for his failure (which was one of supervision and workmanship), and actually billed me for the cost of the sundials of which I had only the ruins – which, in short, I had not got. When I queried this, he maintained that the fault was mine for giving him the job (!) and that I should have known it was beyond him. (His letters never expressed anything but total enthusiasm and extreme confidence.) After an unpleasant row, during which I pointed out that I still had to pay the builder (who did the actual labouring-work on the hillside), and would also have to pay for the removal of the sundials, as well as for the new (replacement) versions (for I am very keen on both sundials) . . it was finally agreed that I would pay only for the drawings and the builder . . and that he would cut a "healing" (sic) version, meanwhile, on the wild stone (which I obtained at my own expense, a quite considerable item).

This is the circumstance in which I am asked to pay, in addition to the charge for cutting the stone, the "travelling time" and "petrol" . . the travelling time alone amounting to one pound less than the total cost of the neon poem 'barque' (which was made in Edinburgh).

I realise that my feelings may be, in part, related to the fact that Sue and I are having particularly severe worries about printing bills at the moment. There is also the endless nerve-destroying niggle of producing things which almost no-one wants, with money one has scarcely got. You know these problems well, so I will not elaborate on them. There remains a feeling that there is some lack of proportion in a man who has a three-day holiday and then bills his host for travelling time, £24. (I am talking, not of the money alone, but of the entire circumstance.)

Now, I am not a mean man. Indeed, I have rarely had enough money to be in a position to aspire to parsimony, far less to practise it. It is a fact, though, that there are times, there are times, when the wear-and-tear of my own struggle – that worm in me – turns, and I can suddenly bear no more of the world's assumption that, since I work for love, and it for money, my money is its own.

No, there are times when I feel that my money – be it a mere tuppence-ha'penny – is my own. And that any person who does not see this on his own account, is in for a shock.

Anyway, the thing is this, that I will (when I can afford it) settle Michael's bill, with the proviso (expressed only to you) that he has settled his hash, as regards further Stonypath holidays, and any other graces and extras (tuppence) which might have been coming his way. (I can't get over certain kinds of vulgarity.) The one step I would like, in the world of action, is to make sure that Michael's visit to you at Canterbury, is not going to be added to the eventual cost of any sundial which is made. If Michael wishes to meet you, well and good – well and very good, for that matter – but I see no reason why he should not pay his own petrol and travelling time, rather than enjoying your hospitality and then billing The Muse (which is what such behaviour amounts to, in the long run). I willingly concede that we all have to live, and to eat, and even have appropriate motorcars and Tv sets . . but I have never got used the idea that hospitality is an exploitable thing.

As you will, I am sure, gather, I am fed-up and hurt. At least one can make sure that future situations don't evolve in a similar way.

At the risk of embarrassing you, may I add that you are one of the people whose unfailing and generous civilisedness is a great compensation for troubles of this sort.

Dash it, one likes to be allowed to be friendly without the underhand worry as to whether it is going to add to the ultimate cost.

The trouble is that MH doesn't see the actual ultimate cost but rather the cash in hand.

This need not alter any of our plans, but I am of the opinion that we should behave in a professional way. (Alas).

Love from us all, as always,

Aye,

Ian

PS John Roberts, the new photographer, has sent a first batch of photos, some of which you may eventually want to use in the catalogue/monograph. They are really splendid photos, & I wonder if you would like me to ask John to prepare some for you to see? (No charge.) More love. (No charge).

Auberge de l'Abbaye
Le Bec-Hellouin
Normandy
25 September [1971]

Dear Ian,

Thank you very much for your letter & for the Wild Hawthorn leaflets. They would have arrived very slightly later than was necessary for my visit to Sweden. But in effect the Swedish backlash (exercised punitively by the auditors of the Swedish parliament) has just begun to fall on the Museum of Modern Art, & as a side-effect of this awesome process I was discouraged from going. I had a long-distance telephone call from the Director's assistant, who conjured up Wagnerian prospects by talking of how 'black' the future looked, & then doubtless returned to the profligate pleasures of Tinguely's porno-kinetic paradise (& the so-called Torpedo Institute, founded for the benefit of young artists desirous of utilising **TECHNOLOGY** . . .).

But I have at least one promising avenue for your splendid prospectus – a fairly wealthy person in the Channel Isles, who just avoided showing me his collection of concrete material in July, & was actually considering publishing a book of 'systematic' poetry in conjunction with my 'Systems' exhibition of English constructive art.[57] (The only reason why he managed to avoid displaying his collection was a combination of his wife's Volkswagen & my personal ankle successively breaking down).

Anyhow, as a result of being spared the voyage to Stockholm, I was able to undertake a more culturally central expedition with Tony to Minster-in-Thanet & the landing place of Hengist & Horsa (if not St Augustine).[58] It

57. I had been meeting throughout the previous year with the 'Systems' group of British constructivist artists who were working towards an exhibition at the Whitechapel Gallery. This opened in March 1972, with my introduction being published in the catalogue, designed by Philip Steadman.

58. The legendary Jutish chieftains Hengist and Horsa, ancestors of the early Kings of Kent, were believed to have landed at Ebbsfleet, on the coast of Thanet, in 449 AD. This was also reputed to be the landing place of St Augustine, on his mission from Rome, in 597 AD.

was one of those late autumn afternoons when the fields are slightly over-ripe with the decay of cabbages, but the warmth of summer seems to linger like a charmed cloud of alcoholic haze over a brandy glass (metaphors borrowed, I fear, from my present unashamed engagement in France, & all that that implies).

I was, by the way, most touched by your favourable impression of Tony. We shall certainly accept the chance of constituting an Arts Council event (& example), provided that the circuit comprises, for the moment, no more than a certain gallery in Lanarkshire & various other places incognito. On a different level, I have felt for some time, & with increasing conviction, that there is a certain complementarity between Tony & myself – on a sort of aesthetic-cultural level – that really can prove in the highest degree beneficial both to ourselves, & possibly, to others. There is, of course, the sense of Tony being very much the man of Southern England while I myself regress continually to the partly barren, partly redolent areas of the Pennine backbone. But there is also the impression of Tony being in so many things, by a kind of inexplicable instinct, right, while I have perhaps to an inordinate degree the kind of flexibility that needs to be measured by a sort of rightness.

Let me point out at this stage, appositely, that he has brought back the most stunning pictures of Stonypath, from really remarkable 'curfew/curlew', 'fragments' sundial, & yachting photos to a veritable Daily-Mirror-holiday-snaps winning record of Eck and Ailie over lunch. (Eck displaying a mouthful of green substances to the camera)

> pls. 13, 12, 1

Michael Harvey has written twice about the proposed Kent sundial. And the fearsome architect has replied to my timid proposal in an encouraging way. So we are quite fairly launched. It seems a good idea to leave open the exact location & type of the sundial until Michael Harvey's visit. (He has, incidentally, offered to illustrate the book of epitaphs which Tony & I intend to publish – an excellent prospect.)

I quite agree to the idea of including the neon poems as a special section of the essay. They provide excellent opportunity for a nostalgic reversion to 'pure' concrete – to the time when there was a global village (& one didn't simply write to one's sister in Brazil).

Better finish now, as my father is almost snoring (tantalising glimpse into the post-prandial world of a Norman Inn)[59] –

Love to Sue, with many thanks for her letter –
& to Eck &Ailie,

Yours

Stephen

Stonypath
14 October [19]71

Dear Stephen,

I have just returned Tony's very pleasant essay, with a letter which contains my comments upon the essay, together with an account – in brief – of our present (and since this seems too exclusive to be accurate, future) misfortunes. Tony, then, will give you some information on these, saving me from having to write the same melancholy paragraphs twice.

I also sent Tony a small gift, which I hope he may share with you; and I mentioned the matter of Concrete Rock, with which you are perhaps already familiar.

I hasten to tell you that we finally heard from Mr Karpel, and he has suggested some complex arrangement – rendered nigh-incomprehensible by his meandering, yet abrupt, prose-style – by which (if we comply with the procedure) we will get back from The Museum, what it cost us to send the things, if one does not count the cost of the box or (of course) our Time. In short, The Museum has – unless I miscalculate – obtained a number of Wild Hawthorn items, for the price of the (so to speak) postage. Or if this is not the case, quite, there has been somewhere that deft twitch of the professional hand, with which I grow familiar. They have the things, and we have not lost an enormous amount more by selling them, than if we had kept them in the cupboard. Such is life.

On the subject of life, I have one piece of good, if sombre, news. It will be recalled – or conveniently forgotten – that my aims in The Fulcrum Affair

59. My excursion to Normandy took place in the company of my father, who recalled walking tours of the province in the 1920s. My mother was recuperating in England from a hip replacement operation.

have been two, firstly, to have it officially confirmed that the book is not a first edition; and secondly to have it withdrawn from public sale. (I do not expect to be able to do much about The Black Market.) Now, it may also be recalled that The Literary World has been pleased (indeed delighted) to say, that I would never get an official statement on the status of the edition . . . and when (thanks to The Parliamentary Commissioner) I had got just such a statement (from The British Museum), it (The Literary World) sagely observed that the statement was valueless since I could never take Fulcrum Press to a court of law.

Here T.L.W. may be right, for it is the government which is going to take Fulcrum Press to court, under the Trade Descriptions Act. The case is already drawn up, and The British Museum has stated that it will be willing, no, eager – to testify in court. Of course, should the Fulcrum book be withdrawn, I will be able to withhold my own evidence, and the case will be dropped.

I have informed Messrs. Rubinstein of this situation, under the heading of 'A Clobber of Circumstances', adding that I discount the rumour that The Royal Navy is even now raising steam.

.

What are we going to do about the (proposed) sundial (or other work) and Michael Harvey and his visit? The time for this is drawing near.

I hope you are fine, Stephen. Aye,

Ian

Canterbury
17 October [1971]

Dear Ian,

It's back to the prodigal use of *20thc. Studies* paper. Not altogether inappropriately, I may add, as on Friday I was made prospective editor – a fearful responsibility, in a situation where we are struggling to increase our meagre circulation.[60] My immediate concern is the forthcoming (light blue) issue on the French New Novel, which will contain my most recent

60. The founding editor, Guido Almansi, had announced his intention of leaving Kent to take up a Chair of Italian at University College Dublin.

justification for the novels of Pinget. The basic conclusion is that Pinget's most recent work is an Apocalypse – beyond which he is not likely to penetrate at least for a substantial time, It is, however, a small-scale Apocalypse – 'Apocalypse de petite semaine'.

Things have moved reasonably well here on several fronts during the opening stages of the term. The local Art College, in the person of its distinctly Scottish principal, is favourable to the idea of a book of epitaphs, & there seems more than a chance that they will be tackling it seriously soon. I had a few words with our University architect & he was most impressed with what I showed him of your collaboration with Michael Harvey – in particular the Biggar Sundial. He had actually come down to Canterbury that very day with the aim of trying out a weather-cock on the Senate House, & is of the opinion that the campus is sorely in need of 'intelligent incident'. He even pointed out a very fine site, which would be splendid for a sundial.

So my next move – as soon as I have spoken to my committee next Thursday – will be to bring in Michael Harvey irrespective of petrol costs. I would at the same time be very grateful to have some idea at this point of what sort of sum represents a possible basis for planning of the work. I think I can see us laying our hands on £300, as a certain minimum. Is it at all likely that a work could be completed & installed, with, of course, fees to yourself and M.H. for not much more than this? Excuse me for asking, but someone will inevitably ask me before long to make an exact calculation, & I would like to be able to give tentative guide-lines.

I wonder if you have heard from Stuart or Ian Gardner of my weekend meeting with Tarasque. I had eventually failed to arrive at the holiday camp, which was perhaps not too bad an idea as there seem to have been periodic fracasses. But Ian Gardner is still participating in the Midland Group exhibition. I very much enjoyed meeting him & seeing more of his work.

I was quite impressed with the plans for the exhibition, & see it really as a way of defining an alternative channel out of the C.P. membership of the mid-60s (a kind of hard-line maintained against Trotskyist revisionism, to carry on the analogy). The selection of prints which they have already prepared will give as clear a picture as possible of the primacy of Wild Hawthorn in this process. And I thought that I should write a catalogue preface which stressed, as it were, the strait & narrow path amid verbi-vocovisual temptations. This would put in a more public context the specific presentation of your work in the Newcastle catalogue.[61]

Simon gives me the impression of being – very properly – shame-faced about his recent criticisms of your work, & didn't in any way repeat them. He & I tramped over vast areas of Notts. in the search for slate headstones, & found some fine examples. Perhaps most eloquent was the otherwise unexceptionable headstone which commemorated the decease (after tribulations) of :

DAFT SHEPHERDS

Everything is rather cold & rainy here. All one can do is to burn lots of logs & stay indoors with one's colds. But Tony, with enormous energy, has completed the first sketch for a decorative scheme that will transform my ½ bedroom (the one built out at the back) into a kind of private chapel. It is a 'Temptation in the Wilderness'.

Looking forward to hearing from you soon – I was really shocked by the passages from the letter that you read out, & only hope it is not a characteristic reaction. Let me counter by saying how much Guido Almansi (ex-Ed. of *20thc. Studies*, professor-elect at Dublin & one of our major luminaries) liked the photos I showed him for the Italian journal. He would very much like to buy copies of the drifter photo, & the one of the marble sundial in the half-distance. Should he write direct to Diane Tammes?

Love to Sue, Eck &Ailie,
Yours

Stephen

Stonypath
20 October 1971

Dear Stephen,

many thanks for your welcome letter, and the Taro, sorry Tarasque, cards. They are both nice, and I especially like the green one, though this is a

61. I had agreed to write an introduction to the Tarasque Press exhibition, entitled *Metaphor and Motif*, which opened at the Midland Group Gallery, Nottingham, in February 1972.

little spoiled by being squint.[62] It occurs (spelling?) to me, that both cards would be greatly enhanced if they were part of a book – if i.e., they were pages. I feel that they need a domain (thus to set off their trellis-enclosed plots). (One could arrange a long walk via the title-page, and subsequent pages, blank, or with small learned Notes. Also, References to me, and to Tony, and other well-known Gardeneers.) What do you think?

William was at that moment in the garden, hatching a trellis-enclosed plot.

A little breeze sprang up. The petals from several nearby bushes fell like a sad Rossetti.

Yes, Ian Gardner had told me of your visit. He gave you a whole paragraph, of extreme enthusiasm. It is a curious feature of Tarasque, that everyone in it, has resigned from it . . and yet it goes on. It is like The Balkans.

DAFT SHEPHERDS is delightful.

The "justification" for Pinget is, that if he had not existed, Ponge would have been forever off-balance.

Here is a little Poem in return for your Postcard:

(daisy)

As regards Canterbury, and the proposed sundial, or work, I should think that £300 or £350 would be adequate. It depends on what we do. As you will recognise, it would be splendid to do my 'wave' –wa~y – poem, (which I am having done domestic-size by Michael Harvey, or was, before The Debt Crisis), as a relief, in black marble, with a little black marble pool. This would (I fear) cost considerably more than £300. Upon the precedent of Biggar (since the architect liked that), it would (from my point of view) be very possible to do a 'Land/Sea' version, in the same black slate, with the same emphasis on the neo-pre-Socratic aspect; and this could look very elegant. It could be as large, and no doubt larger, than the Biggar one. I will suggest a few ideas to Michael Harvey, so that he should come to you equipped with some rough sketches.

62. Tarasque had sent me copies of the two poem cards already shown to Finlay in draft: *Vierzehnheiligen* and *The Garden as a Parenthesis* ('the green one').

> pls. 18, 19

I have proposed to him, as a financial basis, that we would add to the basic costs (not including his time), a sum which gives a reasonable total, and that this (added) sum he and I would half, as our payment.

I will emphasise to Michael (whether he accepts this suggestion or not) that I do not want to exploit the university.

So I will write to Michael in the very near future.

I entirely understand your reluctance to bring in the question of money; it is a miserable matter.

.

About the good Guido, I think he should, yes, write direct to Diane Tammes (14 Cumberland Street, Edinburgh 3), ordering the photos. She has a 'studio' so surely must be used to making copies to order. The only problem may be that of identifying the photos, and this could probably be overcome by G.A. explaining that he saw them as part of the selection made for a French magazine. (She should recall this.)

DAFT PHOTOGRAPHERS

There is little News that is not Bad News, so I will pause here. Love,

Ian

Stonypath
27 October 1971

Dear Stephen,

here is the new 'homage': it is signed on the reverse, or below the waterline. I hope you may like it.[63]

I am hastening to send it just in case you wanted to use it as a reference point in the monograph/catalogue. While the question of its allegorical aspect is to the fore, let me add that the Prinz Eugen had very refined engines, and a very dedicated engineroom crew. It is said that, when she was taken over by the Americans (on the defeat of Germany) eleven of her twelve boilers were in working order; and by the time the Americans had sailed her to Honolulu,

63. The print, *Homage to Gomringer*, was signed on the back by Finlay, and my copy was editioned 3/300. Finlay began to sign prints, and note their edition numbers, around this time.

only one boiler was still in use. The cruiser Concrete Poetry has suffered a similar fate.

Tell me, did you ever hear from the Editor of Ships Monthly? I wrote him again, to remind him that he had not answered your letter . . and this (very pleasant) letter of mine has not been acknowledged. If a man mentions Keats in his Editorials, he had better acknowledge my more amiable letters . . and if he does not, he will deserve what this Editor is about to get. Ships may have Watertight Compartments; Cultures should not. Love,

Ian

Canterbury
15 November [1971]

Dear Ian,

Here I am devoting so much time to writing about you, that I am consistently prevented from writing to you. It is a prepositional anomaly that must obviously be put right. Especially as there is quite a bit of positively interesting news to communicate.

But first of all, let me reply to Sue's twice-made enquiry about the Jersey patron of the arts. He is: Michael Armstrong, Le Haut du Mont, La Haule, Jersey, C.I. He collects books in general, with an inclination towards the 'beau livre' & I think he might well order some items. I'm afraid I only had two copies of the list & have already given one away – so there is nothing to send back.

The Editor of *Fishing Monthly* (*Ships* ditto?) has not replied yet.

Michael Harvey's visit passed off well, I think.[64] I expect he has rung you about it & hope his conclusions are satisfactory. He concluded that he would produce drawings of, in particular, the 'Land's Shadows' – but in lettering closer to the glass poem & hence more directly suitable for slate. Also he said that if you had any new possibility, he could quickly make another design to show us. The committee, such as it is, was quite won over to the project as a whole & it only remains to settle the precise question of the work to be chosen.

64. Michael Harvey had visited the university and examined the proposed site on 12 November.

Michael took several photos of the site which the architect suggested. It is slightly raised, with a newly planted rose-garden just beyond & invokes a distant prospect of Richborough Power Station, which is tantamount to the sea.

We looked ahead & thought late April a good time for installation. I have since looked into a luminous vista which would involve an unveiling by Jo Grimond (our Chancellor)'s wife with her Orkneyan associations & an Open Lecture on your work given by me to all comers, illustrated by colour slides (those taken by Tony in September are really splendid, & perhaps, with the installation in prospect, one could come and take some more?).

I hope the financial question is now settled. Michael expounded his doctrine of relativity in charges, although it was not too clear whether he viewed the University as a parallel to 'Unilever' or 'the chap down the road'. I think we were in agreement that the maximum for the slate and his labour should be £225, the slate being up to £100. I would suggest, as a preliminary estimate, that your fee might be £125, reaching a total of £350. But unexpected circumstances may modify this costing – with the proportions remaining roughly the same.

The monologue is proceeding but not, I hope, degenerating into a monotone. I can probably send it before the weekend. I see it as a small, rather preciously finished book, with vignettes and copious illustrations.[65] Am I being realistic? (Visions of inter-Stellar space)

Could I end for now, in the expectation of catching this evening's post?

One very central point – I hope to mention as a last stage the neon 'barque', the little Sundial booklet so appositely received on Saturday, & the *sails/waves* card. Am I right in thinking the latter to be a neon poem too?

Love to Sue, Eck &Ailie.
Yours

Stephen

65. Despite the confusions that followed, this expectation was broadly fulfilled in the final publication of *Ian Hamilton Finlay: An Illustrated Essay* which was to accompany Finlay's exhibition at the Scottish National Gallery of Art, opening in July 1972 (see pp. 183–86). The press, however, would be Shenval and not Stellar.

Stonypath
25 November [19]71

Dear Stephen,

your essay/monograph arrived safely and I must immediately say that it is most delightful, and undoubtedly marks the New Epoch (of Post-Concrete?). Seriously, it does draw together many threads, and it is interesting to set it beside a letter from Jonathan Williams which came at the same time – a letter touching on the subject of Audience, and noting that The Widest Possible Audience (which we all seek) does not perhaps – cannot perhaps, exist for serious art.

All this we will go into later. I must now confess that I have told Mr Carrell that he can go to H—l and that I want no further part in his f——g exhibition. Like all such stories, this is a complicated one; but the root of it lies in the fact (which dawned on me like a Sodden Twilight) that exhibitions now exist only for the Arts Council and the Impresarios and Directors who get handed public money to put them on. They have nothing to do with the poet or artist, who alone gets no payment, and who has to manage as best he can in the little cracks left by the ineptitude of this new breed of con-men – who (one notes) know nothing about culture and know **LESS** about organisation – who are **HUMAN JELLY-BABIES*** [*green ones, to boot] (if you know those sweeties) **ALL**.

Anyway, here is your splendid essay and where are the photographs that were supposed to be available? Half of them don't yet exist. For some five months I have been patiently reminding both the photographer and Mr Carrell, that the photos would be needed to illustrate your text, and that November would be the deadline if we are to have the book ready for the exhibition. When I ask where the photos are, the photographer assures me that Mr Carrell's most recent (John Furnival) catalogue publication, was put to the printer two weeks before it was needed – so what am I worrying about? There is a whole 5 months to spare.

Oddly enough, I feel that I have reached the stage, and that you have reached the stage, where endeavours are not going to be put through the fine mesh of **THICK DOLTS** – rather say, shout, **HURL**, a Carlylean **NAY**. (that is intended to read Carlyle-ean.)

Likewise, I am informed that my little Fifties and Zulus film is to be part of the exhibition. But where is the film? The cameraman (much recommended by Mr Carrell) not only did not make the film, but stole the money that was advanced to make it . . . and of course it would be uncivilised and unthinkable to pursue the fuckpig to London and get the money back – easier by far to make the film fit the depleted budget: THAT'S the civilised way. (one would think that the cameraman, because he has stolen the money without FUSS, is the Shining Example in the whole affair).

However, says Mr Carrell, Stirling will now advance further money and they see no reason why the film of the wee boats should not now be made, in time for May. I would see no reason either, had I not been reflecting, only yesterday, on the potentialities for ice-yachting at Stonypath, and on the odd capacity of ice to resemble some particularly stubborn sort of plastic, lasting on and on, through Freeze and Thaw. – All summer and autumn I TOLD and TOLD these wretched people, that if there was to be a film, action was needed – but action – AH, that is something which must be postponed till the Last Minute has become Too Late.

Yes, the work of art is the LAST thing to be considered; the work of art is what must be squeezed, crushed, mangled, till it fits the tiny space left by ineptitude and laziness. Anything will do so long as the Account-Books can solemnly record that <u>an exhibition took place</u>.

Stirling also supposes that it is to be supplied with the book of the music of the film – which has not been made.

It looks well in writing. It sounds well in Directorial Confabs. True, it is the sheerest fantasy, but what of that?

Those who favour the two-week-before-publication method, of Mr Carrell, might reflect on the fact that Mr J[onathan] Williams recently brought me a fascinating Ceolfrith leaflet referring to one <u>Basis</u> Bunting – and Big J also told me that the 2-weeks-is-ample-time catalogues, had to be rushed to the exhibition as in some early Saturday serial (spelling?) and that only 20 or something were ready at all – which is not to my taste.

So, dear Stephen, I write in the Centre of this Storm. I expect I will still have to hear from Stirling. We will see what happens. WHATEVER HAPPENS I do assure you that your text will be published and that your work has not been wasted. If need be I will make alternative plans. What I CANNOT do is to throw your most Christian prose to these hyenas . . . nor can I tolerate their nonsense longer, I just have to explode.

This is an interim letter. Both Sue and I think your essay delightful. I will write less heatedly later (I hope). Meanwhile, let me at those Long Boats . . .

Love,

Ian

Canterbury
26 November [19]71

Dear Ian,

Here is a section on the neon-poems to go in the original essay. It is to be inserted before the last paragraph, as will be clear, I am sure. Hope it is also useful for Demarco.

Good to hear you last night – the idea of doing the book with Stuart [Mills] is a much more attractive one! Did you find the sun-dial situation promising?

Yours

Stephen

Stonypath
27 November [19]71

Dear Stephen,

thank you so much for the essay-insert, on the neon-poems, which arrived safely today, and which I will add to the essay, and type out for the Demarco Gallery, with some suitable heading.

I remain in sombre mood, living not only amid The Storms of Sunderland (which does not storm), <u>and</u> in the margin of our debts . . which somehow prevent all peaceful as well as creative thought. (I dare not start a new poem with any printer or manufacturer, carver or whatever.)

Except, of course, Michael will continue with The Canterbury Sundial. Yes indeed, the arrangements outlined in your letter, seem fine, and fit perfectly with my own conclusions. Michael wrote very recently that he has not yet prepared any new sketches of 'Land's Shadows', but that he will. (I have suggested that we might combine the green slate, unpolished, with the sunpath and net-names (only) in dull aluminium* [*a slightly raised, separate grid] – the larger, or main, letters being carved. Michael seems to approve of this idea.)

I am not against submitting further ideas, but there is a certain danger in feeling that a new work must be better than an old, as-yet unrealised one, simply because it has the edge of the new . . which the old yet retains for other people. What do you think? (What I mean is, that opportunities are so rare, that one is tempted to hop from idea to idea, to cram several years of pints into one Canterbury pot . . . . But we should certainly change the project if there is any good reason.)

I had to 'phone Stuart the other night, and I mentioned to him the possibility of replacing the text in his proposed book, with yours. As I suspected he had not yet begun his text, and he seems to be awaiting a loan* [*grant?] from The Scottish Arts Council, to be confirmed (he hopes) in January. His idea is to do a book in the same format as the little Max Bill, and Stellar have estimated a cost of £700.

The S. Arts Council are apparently aware of this.

I see – not least in the middle of the night – certain Worries in the project, and I wonder whether you feel that we (you and I) could manage them together. My first Worry – leaving Sunderland/Stirling aside – is, that Stuart is (I speak in confidence but say nothing which can be unknown to you) in many ways as unreliable as Mr Carrell. Neither (for example) goes in for proof reading. Again, Tarasque is not exactly efficient, in that a great deal seems to fall between the 2 stools of Simon and Stuart . . a consideration which is not made less sombre by the qualification that Simon and Stuart are not the only 2 stools, there being the cosmic Anneira, and the delightful Rosemary. (Less liable to cause us rue.) To give an example of what I mean, I recently had a quite agonised letter from one of my fans (I have 3, in the country), (and 5 in the world), explaining that my Autumn List says that The Weed Boat Masters Ticket Part One may be obtained from Tarasque, and that 2 letters had produced no response whatever . . And what should he do . . . And it is a fact that we get frequent letters lamenting Tarasque's silences, our explanation (from Stuart) always being that he thought Simon had attended to the matter . . . Which raises another problem, Simon, for it would not be possible to BEAR the thought of Simon sending off the monograph, EVER, AT ALL. (I recently got a large packet of Simon's things, from an American bookshop: Simon had sent them without explanation or covering note, or return address . . . so (as I wrote to the shop, in explanation) it was a case of the Sins of the Son being Visited Upon The Father.)

Anyway: do you think we could draw up some kind of contract with Stuart, giving us a veto right to intervene and restore Order, silence Simon, (did you get his recent mimeod communication?) . . . and see that the book is sold?

(I have the Wild Thought that **THE** solution would be if The Arts Councils gave **ME** the money which they give to such as Carrell, to act for me, on the grounds that I have been seen to act, and publish, and proof read, where all these others have been seen to . . . . . But we need not go into all that . .)

What – being realistic – for your optimism is not in doubt, dear Stephen --- do you think? Could the thing be done?

The other main Worry is, that Stuart would have to agree to supplement his photos with other illustrations (referred to in your text). I don't know if he realises this. He was very keen on the idea of using your text, but he is also very keen on his photos: so that could be a snag. We will have to ascertain his feelings.

.

Stirling (MacRoberts Arts Centre), which was putting up £500 towards the book and exhibition, has not (of course) answered my letter, preferring to be in touch with Mr Carrell, on the assumption (I presume) that he knows more about (say) my wee film than I do – this kind of assumption being quite instinctive in people who dispense public money to the Arts.

He will shortly (the Stirling chap) get A Definitive Statement of my Position, by Precarious First-Class Post. He has a loch so he can expect a long ship.

I really do like your Monologue very much, Stephen. I am most truly sorry that there is being all this cafuffle, with what Richard Demarco (in a mimeod communication in today's post) calls, 'The Magical World of Christopher Carrell'.

Did it ever strike you that the Long Boat is in The Eye of The Beholder? I mean, could there, perchance, be an Arts Council Monastery which sees the Wild Hawthorn as a Long Boat?

Perish the thought.

Or the Arts Council.

Or The Magical World of Christopher Carrell.

Love,

Ian

Stonypath
19 December [19]71

Dear Stephen,

here are the *Seashells*; I do hope you like them.

The tube for your Christmas Present Proper, is (alas) still on its way from London. I hope you will forgive the delay. Meanwhile, we all wish you a very happy Christmas.

Love,

Ian

Clough House
Almondbury
Huddersfield
21 December [19]71

Dear Ian,

Thank you so much for your letter, arrived a good few days ago, & for the two delightful cards which were waiting for me here at home.[66] I expect a suspiciously bulky parcel will have been deposited by now in the interests of Eck and Ailie – it will be followed by a slim and sinister parcel for Sue and yourself full of materials not imaginatively unconnected with German Concrete. Something to accompany the battleship era . . .

I did of course also receive the letter (copy of) to Christopher Carrell.[67] I expect that is where the matter stands now. As for the possibility of a book with Stuart, I do feel there is a significant difference between the general, non-particularised projects (e.g. *Tarasque*) & the personally significant ventures. No doubt because there are less stools to fall between, the individual Tarasque productions seem generally free of the baleful influence of Miss Print. Perhaps the way of ensuring correct proof reading etc. would therefore

66. The two cards were the Finlays' own Christmas card, 'Xmas Morn', and a Christmas card issued as a greeting by Daedalus Press, 'The Land's Shadows'. Both were designed by Michael Harvey.

67. I had received a copy of the letter written to Christopher Carrell on 9 December 1971, in which Finlay listed the various issues raised in our correspondence that had led him to withdraw from the proposed exhibitions at Newcastle and Stirling.

be to place the ball unequivocally, so to speak in Stuart's court – & of course to insist on our own partnership in the various stages.

But, of course, what you say of the possibly divergent subject matter of my essay & Stuart's photos may raise difficulties also. It would, in all ways, be more realistic a prospect if you were in control –

Before I begin more general news, I should mention two distinct enquiries from friends which will undoubtedly result in WHP orders. First of all, one of our Kent colleges (named after the redoubtable Lord Keynes) is interested in buying a few prints. I have suggested that, rather than risk the inconvenience of ordering by post, those concerned could look at the works which I have & decide on that basis. This is what they will be doing.

Secondly, I had a pleasant overnight stay with Reg Gadney – whom you will remember – & he said he would like to place a standing order. I should think that in the present situation it would be more profitable for him to get at least a selection of the recent work, which is so plentiful and excellent. Anyhow I said I would ask you to send a catalogue (if you still have copies) & possibly to draw up a (possible) short list of works. I suppose I have in mind a kind of:

CHRISTMAS HAMPER FOR THE
~EPICURE~

> Contents: 1 'Little Seamstress' (genuine marzipan only); set of 6 shells (boned, dissected & served in aspic jelly); 1 Rock Rose (finest crystallised variety) . . . etc.

Just to recall – as it had unaccountably slipped my mind – the Shenval Print is quite terrific. So much better than any of their previous offerings & quite perfect as an object – in its multifold promise.[68]

I was visiting Reg to hand over the mss of my 'Art & artistic groups', which has reached its conclusion in a combination of critical rigour & thinly veiled satire.[69] There is such an overblown pomposity about so many of our contemporary (post-war) phenomena, when it is seriously maintained that for [Claes] Oldenburg to construct a 60 ft. ice-pack that wobbles is a marriage of art & technology.

68. Shenval Press had excelled themselves in commissioning Finlay to compose their folding 'Christmas Poem Print', with drawings by Ron Costley.

69. This short book, intended for a series to be edited by Reg Gadney for Paladin Books, was never published.

If I go to Paris in the New Year, I shall avoid Francis Bacon & all his works (nearly all, at any rate)[70] confining myself to Léger & just conceivably early Picasso.

I get occasional queries from my committee about the Canterbury sundial, & hope we can consider the final drawings early next term. As far as I can see, there is no obstacle at the moment & it should be possible to envisage an April installation.

I shall be settling down to a Christmas of honest toil & agreeable diversion. My first literary treat, consumed in an afternoon of travel from London to Yorkshire, was [Robert Louis Stevenson's] *Weir of Hermiston* & my present sequel is Kipling's *Limits & Renewals*. But there is the sterner stuff of a French volume on the theory of painting, which has begun with indigestible pronouncements emanating ultimately from Marx & proposes to continue with 'Matisse's system'.[71]

But before essaying either of these possibilities, I must wish you all a very happy Christmas in unaccustomed mildness & hope to hear from you soon (I'm here till 1 January, then Canterbury, with an excursion to Paris) –

Yours

Stephen

70. There was a major retrospective exhibition of Bacon's paintings at the Grand Palais, Paris, which closed on 10 January 1972.

71. My review of Marcelin Pleynet's *L'Enseignement de la peinture* (1971), a study largely concerned with Matisse, was published in *TLS* 3664 (19 May 1972) under the title 'The Vanguard of the Modern Movement'.

January 1972

On my return from Paris in the New Year, I received a phone call from Stonypath in which Finlay suggested that the Canterbury sundial should not be based on his poem 'The Land's Shadows', as we were planning. It should take the simpler form of the 'Land/Sea' poem, originally published in 1967, in a freehand poem/print version designed by Herbert Rosenthal. The new version, using classic carved lettering, had already been tested as a prototype for the experiments in cast concrete undertaken the previous June – Finlay's disastrous 'Stonypath Sundial Week' (see pp. 142–3). There was rapid agreement between Finlay, myself and Michael Harvey on the suitability of this change of plan. The material for the sundial was to be green slate, as already established.

Stonypath
11 January [19]72

Dear Stephen,

it was grand to hear you on the 'phone, and I was very cheered to know that 'Land/Sea' is not ruled out. The more I considered Michael's photo of the site, the more I felt that 'Land/Sea' was the answer, both in terms of the possibilities and of the limitations. It is a poem which can acknowledge, and use, bleakness, and which will contrive to be elegant and classical, while tolerating those buildings in the middle-distance. I do hope this estimate is not over-optimistic, but I gave the problem a lot of thought, to the point where a growing feeling became indistinguishable from conscience. There is the additional advantage that you will perhaps share these views, and feel able to explain them to the committee. I have asked Michael to consider my (quite detailed) suggestions, and, if he approves them, to go on and prepare the more detailed drawings. The material I have suggested is polished green slate.

Are there motorcars in the vicinity?

The other Practical Matter – is the adjective too optimistic? – of the catalogue/book, is in active abeyance (if you will accept that category, or state, as a possibly valid one). I have suggested to the chastened Mr Carrell that he and Douglas Hall, should discuss the proposed exhibition, and then tell me the terms they can offer. I will keep the ms meanwhile, and when there is some solid sort of hope, we can discuss the minor amendments which are all it needs. I hope this paragraph does not depress you, and I will not (of course) make any final arrangements without discussing with you. (Incidentally, D. Hall was asking to see the ms, and I have so far adjudged that he might not be entirely pleased with certain (very objective) comments in the early section.)

Perhaps you could write a wee note to Shenval, saying you like the print, which I do think is jolly nice.[72]

That will be super if Keynes College buy some prints. I suppose you have most Wild H. things there; if you are lacking anything, just let me know.

That is super that Reg Gadney (the very name is like a bell,[73] or at least the honk of a Duck of yesteryear), would like a standing order. I am not at all sure of the address we have for Reg, (addresses rarely last long in these hectic modern days, **HMD**'s) , and if you could send his present address, we will send a list (catalogue) and suggested Selection of Earlier Works.

Fancy your 'Art and artistic groups' being complete. Does it include the redoubtable Glasgow Boys? (Hurray, hurray, we are the Glasgow Boys/Hurray, hurray, we are the Glasgow boys/From Anderston to Maryhill we splash the paint with poise/Preparing the way for Robin Philipson . . .)[74]

My neon show is now over, and the poems are back at Stonypath, lacking only the plugs, which I expect were purloined by the young lady who took over the room with her 3D photos . . or are they 5D, (I forget). Your little paragraphs were splendidly prophetic, for *The Scotsman* dismissed the exhibition in a single sentence, noting that the medium has commercial associations . . and giving much praise to the ceramic cameras dangling on parachutes, which dominated the stairs. (These were by a 'promising' student.)

72. Shenval Press had produced a folding print by Finlay ('The Flower of the Fal') as their Christmas greeting.

73. Quotation from the last stanza of John Keats's 'Ode to a Nightingale': for Reg Gadney's correspondence with Finlay in the 1960s, see *Midway*, passim.

74. Finlay is evoking the chant of a notorious Protestant gang which had operated in a suburb of Glasgow in the 1920s: 'Hurrah! Hurrah! We are the Billy Boys/Hurrah! Hurrah! We make a lot of noise.' 'Billy' refers to the Protestant King William III. Sir Robin Phillipson, President of the Royal Scottish Academy 1973–83, was noted for his bold use of colour.

The whole thing was very unsatisfactory and I shall not bother to exhibit at the Demarco Gallery again, and shall only (indeed) exhibit, in future, when there is some definite recompense for me, in the form of a large grant to produce the works, a catalogue/book, or whatever . . Where galleries are entirely subsidised by the Arts Council, their interest is in having the works, but not in selling them (about which they could not care less).

It was kind of you to wish us a Christmas of "unaccustomed mildness" and unfortunate that it turned out to be one of unaccustomed illness instead. It is perhaps the only Christmas Day on which I have ever had precisely what I wanted for my Dinner, (a cup of hot water), and I am still pondering that reversal of things which allowed everything to smell of food except food, which smelled of old fog. My bedside was dominated by the Christmas Tree, and it was certainly the Christmas of the birds-eye-view, through encroaching needles. I must not leave this subject without recording a delightful example of Communication or Interpretation. A feature of this Flu was, that one was unable to sleep, and tended to welcome the first glint of dawn by tottering to the kitchen, to fill a hot-bottle and make a delicious drink of hot water. Sue's father apparently behaved just as I did, and it was reported by Sue's mother that he "seemed to be much better and had been up before anyone else, making his own breakfast", though he had gone back to bed now.

Well, Stephen, Festive seasons cannot last forever and I have to remind you that Exam Time is here again; you have some Questions to answer, or Answer, and will find them enclosed. I will be very pleased to hear how you get on.[75]

Love from us all – and I hope Paris was very satisfactory (even if, alas, foreign),

Aye,

Ian

Enigmatic PS: have you encountered d'arcy-kaye as yet?

75. *THE WEED BOAT MASTERS TICKET* Preliminary Test (Part Two). Drawings by Ian Gardner. Printed by hand in Scotland at the Salamander Press. (Q.1: Distinguish between (a) the windfalls of Appledore and (b) the landfalls of Appledore). My copy was inscribed 'To the Skeely [i.e. skilful] Skipper from Master Finlay, 1972'.

The arrangements for the completion of Finlay's first public commission outside Scotland continued methodically throughout 1972. On 30 January, Michael Harvey wrote to me about the need to order the slab of green slate, and suggested that we might 'go for a fine rubbed finish which will bring out the colour of the slate without being shiny'. On 16 March, the University Surveyor wrote to me, conveying the University Architect's approval of the design, and suggesting that there should be agreement reached on the precise placing of the sundial. On 10 April, Harvey wrote to me again, noting that the carved slate slab had been delivered to the university in the previous week, and sending detailed drawings for its installation. The arrangements for the concrete blocks that were cast to support the slab, and the surrounding paving, were worked out at the university in the course of the summer. During much of the Autumn term I was absent on study leave which I spent mainly in Paris. On 26 December 1972, however, Finlay wrote to thank me for sending 'the first Canterbury sundial photos'. He commented: 'I do think the sundial looks very good, and having expected the worst of the site, I am really most pleasantly surprised. That particular "table" form of sundial, does tend to fit in well, on almost any site.'

A quasi-official inauguration took place in mid-January 1973, on a weekend when the Chancellor of the University, Jo Grimond, had invited a predominantly Scottish group of visitors to Canterbury to discuss the future of Art Education. The guests included the painter Alastair Flattely, then Principal of Gray's School of Art in Aberdeen; James Naughtie, the future radio journalist (then President of the Students Union at Aberdeen University); the collage artist and Head of Fine Art at Brighton Polytechnic, Gwyther Irwin; and Richard Demarco. Finlay commented in his letter of 16 January 1973: 'I was delighted to have your letter, with the realistic account of the staggeringly improbable gathering around The Canterbury Sundial. Naughtie, Flattely, and Demarco . . . Grimond, Irwin . . . No, no, it is too improbable.'

Friday 14 January [1972]
Canterbury

Dear Ian,

It's good to know you have all recovered from the 'flu. It really is one of Life's capital injustices that a family living the healthy outdoor life on a wind-swept hillside (!) should be periodically visited by Oriental bugs while peripatetic persons hopping from one sink of iniquity to another should remain relatively immune (I suppose the latter develop *anti-bodies*).

The latest sink was, of course, Paris. I managed to see a succession of friends, including Frank Popper (now announcing the autumn publication of our combined *Agam*)[76] & Bernard Lassus – centre of a delightful family among whom Antoine, aged 12, insisted on posing to me the flattering question: 'Stéphen, comment fait-on pour devenir gentleman?' (Sue, please translate!). Of Bernard Lassus, more later.

I must thank you once again for the splendid collection of *Sea-Shells* – also for the *Weed-Boat Master* pt. 2 which arrived yesterday with your very welcome letter. The imagination is working covertly on the questions (like our new-style exams, it is a 'thirty-day paper', I should hope). By a sideways stretch of connotations not to be explained, that evokes the subject of *Tarasque* and the Tarasque exhibition. I hope you approve of the enclosed introduction to that approaching event, a piece not devoid of an anti-individualising humour (as E. J. might put it).[77]

I sympathise with the difficulty of showing the Ceolfrith Essay to the Scottish Arts Council! But it is fine that Chris Carrell is chastened, & altogether right that you should be making your own terms. I am of course willing to let the essay go wherever you think appropriate. But I might outline a possibility that is also opening up – one that is entirely compatible with its appearance in catalogue form. I have decided to approach a publisher (Studio Vista in the first instance) with a proposal for a collection of essays provisionally (& lamely) entitled 'Essays towards Post-Modernism'. It would be composed mainly of already existing essays, which have appeared in foreign languages, truncated form etc. The present order seems to be:

1. Introduction – Critical theory and practice (Ruskin, Morris, Pater: Formalism, Structuralism) – need for *integrative* and *penetrative* criticism

2. (Thackeray) 'Anti-history of Henry Esmond'

3. 'The rewards of Kipling'

4. 'Robert Pinget: the end of a modern way'

76. This proved to be an over-optimistic estimate (see also p. 140).

77. This was a proof of my Introduction to the catalogue of the imminent Tarasque Press exhibition at the Midland Group Gallery, Nottingham. The arcane phrase 'not devoid of an anti-individualising humour' is borrowed not in fact from E[rnst J[andl] but from another 'phonic' poet, Paul de Vree, whose work had been published alongside that of Jandl in *Form* 3 ((December 1966), pp. 22–23. Finlay had quoted it as one of the captions to photographs of fishing boats in his *Ocean Stripe* 5 (Tarasque Press, 1967).

5. 'Bernard Lassus & classical space'

6. 'Ian Hamilton Finlay'

7. 'The Systems Group & the constructive tradition'

8. Documenta 1972 – retrospect

***

I see it as a place of fruitful *convergences*, & hope at least to convince someone else of the notion – what do you think? (I'll explain at greater length when I have a full summary).

Yes, I do know D'A*rcy K*aye & I also have received this morning The *Loco Logo-Daedalist.*[78] They both seem to me indigestible, albeit fascinating (not that my digestion may not be too delicate). All the same, I can think of elucidating D'A.K. in a positive way, while *LLD* is frankly baffling (though *sympathetic* in the extreme).

I shall drop this into the pm. post if I stop now. By the way, Tony is having his 21st birthday next Friday (21 Jan.) & would, I'm certain, appreciate a colourful word –

Love to Sue, Eck &Ailie
Yours

Stephen

As indicated in the two foregoing letters, the fate of my 'Ceolfrith essay' (so-called because it had been originally commissioned for the projected Finlay exhibition at the Ceolfrith Gallery, Sunderland) was hanging in the balance as Finlay negotiated a change of venue with two Scottish galleries. In part through the decisive intervention of Douglas Hall, Director of the Scottish National Gallery of Modern Art in Edinburgh, a solution was eventually found. This Gallery was situated at the time in the fine eighteenth-century building of Inverleith House, in the midst

78. 'D'Arcy Kaye' was the pseudonym of Robert Kenedy, a librarian working at the Victoria & Albert Museum, who had published a version of Apuleius's *Golden Ass* with Calder and Boyars in 1964, and was a strong supporter of Finlay's work. *D'Arcy Kaye's Chapter One*, published by The Acorn Press, purported to be a Chinese translation of the first chapter of Kenedy's epic poem. *The Loco Logo-Daedalist in situ* was the title of the newly published edition of work by Finlay's old friend, the American poet Jonathan Williams.

of the Scottish National Botanic Garden. Hall combined with Northern Arts and the University of Stirling to sponsor an exhibition that would open in Edinburgh (8 July 1972), and then travel to Stirling and Newcastle. My 'illustrated essay' was the text for the catalogue.

Finlay had questioned in his letter of 11 January whether my relatively harsh comments on the earlier treatment of his work by Scottish critics would prove acceptable in the context. In the event, the essay was published without any modifications. The extract that follows is the first of the four sections contained in the essay, and was my attempt to sum up the critical issues that appeared at the time to be raised by this showing of Finlay's work. Although my argument dwelled of necessity upon the trials of previous years, the appearance of this catalogue in fact marked a turning point. For the first time, Finlay's multifarious achievement was presented to the public in the sympathetic setting of a major national institution.

One of Ian Hamilton Finlay's recent works is a screen-print entitled 'Homage to Gomringer'. The heavy cruiser *Prinz Eugen* is sketched out against the neutral grey background, calling to mind the comparable profile of a full-rigged ship in the screen-prints predecessor 'Homage to Mozart'. Eugen Gomringer, progenitor of the European movement of Concrete poetry, is identified with the immaculate design of the modern warship just as the strains of Mozart could be identified with the billowing rococo forms of the sailing ship. But there is also an allegory underpinning the use of *Prinz Eugen* at this juncture. When its dedicated German crew handed over the warship at the end of the Second World War, ten out of eleven engines were working. But by the time that the Americans had sailed *Prinz Eugen* to Honolulu, only one of these was still in operation. The same thing has happened, Finlay implacably infers, to the 'Cruiser Concrete poetry'.

It would be disingenuous to begin any account of Finlay's work over the last decade without paying attention first of all to the polemical intention which such an interpretation implies. It is not the whole story, and for the most part my study will attempt to place Finlay's various directions of activity against a background which is emphatically not that of the immediate moment. But the history of his protracted dispute with the Fulcrum Press over the publication of *The Dancers Inherit the Party*, the motive that lies behind the notional launching of his 'Wild Hawthorn Kite' for a leaflet raid on the Arts Council of Great Britain, and above all the anomaly which lies behind his identification with a direction of literary activity which now almost totally fails to correspond to his own aims and ideals – all of these factors belong to the foreground of his significance as an exemplary artist. It would be possible to hold that the recuperative methods practised by society to ensure the survival and acceptance of its original yet uncompromising artists have reached a peak of technical efficiency. Yet, as with the not entirely dissimilar question of aid to underdeveloped countries, questions must continue to be posed about the actual effects of public patronage. It would be foolish to deny that artists of value receive necessary grants from the public purse, and even the most uncompromising may occasionally find himself within this company. Yet it also undeniable that such public patronage amounts to neither a genuine recognition by the public, nor the implication that the artists so favoured measure up to any identifiable criterion of quality. The price of recuperation is therefore a cultural pluralism. And it is within this dilemma that Finlay clearly stands.

What I originally referred to as a polemical attitude should perhaps be more clearly defined in terms of an overall critical attitude. Finlay's inability to accept a situation of compromise is based not so much on the tactics of a short-term commitment as on the overall aesthetic strategy which he employs throughout his work. At a period when much of the vigour of literary polemic is spent, not to say wasted, on questions of morality and machinery, like the issue of censorship, Finlay strikes the wildly uncharacteristic posture of an artist whose primary, but insistent, concern is with the exactness of form. His whole course of activity could in fact be seen as a critique of the language of forms, the cultural treasury, as it has been received from the past. And, of course, this critique extends inevitably to the present.

We are therefore obliged to reckon with the bizarre paradox that Finlay is too exclusively preoccupied with the critique of forms to be wholly recognisable as a contemporary artist. We are familiar with the artist who develops as a surrogate personality some clearly identifiable angle on social and moral affairs, but an entire and exclusive commitment to art is a disturbing phenomenon. Moreover Finlay is involved in a field of activity that extends over the entire spectrum of language and design, and, as a result, he is only with difficulty accepted as a contributor to the particular, familiar spheres of poetry, painting and sculpture. Lastly, and perhaps most strangely of all, his position as a Scottish artist, which provides the clue to so much of his work, is a perpetual source of confusion and misunderstanding. This is partly because, in terms of the accepted image of Concrete poetry, the concrete poet has abandoned his national affiliations to gain an international *persona.* But it is also because of the apparent failure of the Scottish Press and the Scottish

Artist, not to mention the Scottish critics and cultural commentators, to see what is distinctively and valuably Scottish in Finlay's work.

This is the general conspectus of a cultural scene which, for reasons that are in a sense not difficult to identify, will not allow Finlay to assume his appropriate stature within the British Isles. Yet his reputation outside Britain hardly makes up for this neglect. The implication of the *Prinz Eugen* print is to criticise the soft internationalism of the 1960s, which, as a result of a series of ever more tenuously based exhibitions of 'visual poetry', reached the utter banality of a recent manifestation where the words 'concrete poetry' were inserted in sticks of rock. It is easy to see many things that are admirable in the view of international poetic brotherhood that sprang from the festivals of the 1960s, of which the Albert Hall bonanza was the precursor. But it is difficult to see any substantial dividends in the field where genuine international contacts had at first been at a premium, that of Concrete poetry itself. Indeed the movement which flowered in Britain in the mid-1960s seems to have gone to seed as a result of the heavy fertilisation of exhibitions and publications. The slight but real virtues of the early work seen in aggregate are unlikely to be recaptured.

Finlay has therefore retreated, if such be the right description, to a position more recognisably national. The orientation of his earlier work towards such points of reference as Suprematism and Fauvism – to take the parameters of his first collection *Rapel* – can be seen as a necessary beating of the aesthetic bounds. They in no way indicate the kind of cultural promiscuity that many present-day artists accept as a fact of their situation. Finlay's concern has always been to establish aesthetic constants, and the utility of the reference to Fauvism and Suprematism lies for him precisely in their degree of contrast, in the fact that they establish a polarity. Throughout the course of his enquiry, he has presumed this underlying ground of aesthetic principle, against which the citation of disparate styles must be measured. His concern, in short, has been with the discovery of classical constants through a progressive review of the absolutes of style.

It needs to be reiterated that this attitude is very far from diminishing the Scottish element in his work. In a situation where, since the late nineteenth century, Scottish painting has been most characteristically associated with a fortuitous derivative of Impressionism, Finlay recovers the classical balance that was a feature of earlier periods. While it may be reasonable to applaud the signs of the 'auld alliance' recurring in the works of prominent painters of the Edinburgh school, this can hardly be taken as a justification for the neglect of an artist who inclines towards the more delicate view of French classicism represented by an Allan Ramsay. In the circumstances we may take it as particularly appropriate that the Scottish National Gallery of Modern Art, itself a fine classical building set in splendid gardens, should be one of the sponsors of the present exhibition. For it is in such a setting, precisely, that the stone inscriptions of Finlay assert their rightful place. The American poet Jonathan Williams has described Finlay as the most significant Scottish designer since Charles Rennie Mackintosh. Let us hope that the general realisation of this unique status will not, as in the case of Mackintosh, be painfully and unreasonably delayed.

WORKS BY IAN HAMILTON FINLAY

With references to the correspondence[1]

I. Works installed in Public Places

The Biggar Sundial ('Azure & Son') 1970: 79–81, 83–4, 134, 143, 154, 156, 163

The Canterbury Sundial ('Land/Sea') 1972: 47, 51, 141, 143, 150, 154, 158, 160, 162–3, 165, 167, 171, 177, 180

II. Works installed at Stonypath (in chronological order of reference)

Sundial ('Fragments/Fragrance'), stone, with Maxwell Allan & Sons: 30, 160

KY, concrete versions: 30, 35, 145

KY (small version), cast iron, painted orange: 54

Rose-lore Bench ('There Is No Rose Without A Thorn'), Caithness stone, with Vincent Butler: 30, 52

The Four Seasons as Fore-and-Afters, wooden (oak) sundial, with John R. Thorpe: 42

Pinnate Evergreen, plant name-tag by engraver from Botanic Gardens, Glasgow: 59–60, 62

True Vine, sundial (Bowl of Ahaz sundial), stone, with Maxwell Allan & Sons: 63, 71

Evening/Sail ('Evening will come'), sundial, wood, with John R. Thorpe: 105, 146

1. The references (to page numbers) are mainly to installed or published works. But they also indicate significant mentions of works still in the planning stage (such as the Canterbury Sundial) and writings discussed, but not yet published, over the time-scale of the correspondence.

Be in Time Fruitful Vine, wooden sundial, with red painted metal gnomon, with John R. Thorpe and Michael Harvey: 138

Bring Back the Birch, stone with carved birch leaves and inscription, with Michael Harvey: 143

The Sea's Waves, tree-bench, wood (oak), with Vincent Butler: 143

Land/Sea, sundial, inscribed wild stone, with Michael Harvey: 150, 157

Tristram's Sail, sundial, circle of slate on rusticated stone base, with Michael Harvey: 153–4

Curfew-Curlew, inscribed wild stone, with Vincent Butler: 160

III. Books and Booklets

Wave, hand-printed at the Salamander Press, 1969: 26, 165

Lanes, drawings by Margot Sandeman, hand-printed at the Salamander Press, 1969: 34, 37, 41

Rhymes for Lemons, with Margot Sandeman, hand-printed at the Salamander Press, 1970: 54–5

Fishing News News, concertina, drawings by Margot Sandeman, hand-printed at the Salamander Press, 1970: 92–3, 102

Ceolfrith 5, with photographs by Diane Tammes, Bookshop Gallery, Sunderland, Ceolfrith Press, 1970: 103, 116

Allotments, visualised by Ian Gardner, poems by Ian Hamilton Finlay, Stuart Mills and Simon Cutts, Tarasque Press, 1970: 145

30 Signatures to Silver Catches, cover drawing by Margot Sandeman, published by Tarasque Press, printed by Shenval Press, 1971

Poems to Hear and See, The Macmillan Company, New York, USA, 1971: 59, 130

A Sailor's Calendar, with Gordon Huntly, Something Else Press, New York, USA, 1971, with interleaves and ring binding: 72, 119

The Olsen Excerpts, photographs by Diane Tammes, Verlag Udo Berger, Göttingen, Germany, 1971: 144–5, 151

A Memory of Summer, with Jim Nicholson, 1971

From 'An Inland Garden', drawings by Ian Gardner, 1971

Evening/Sail 2, with Michael Harvey, 1971, screenprint by Girdwood: 146

The Weed Boat Master's Ticket Preliminary Test (Part Two), drawings by Ian Gardner, printed by hand at the Salamander Press, 1971: 179, 181

IV. Cards and Folding Cards

Skylarks, folding card, 1969: 56, 66–7, 69, 88, 90–91

Valses pour Piano (Water Music), 1970

Arcadian Sundials, with Margot Sandeman, folding card, 1970

From *'The Metamorphoses of Fishing News'*, 1970: 55

A Waterlily Pool (h'arbour), with Ian Gardner, 1970: 59, 60

Still Life with Lemon, 1970: 68

Azure & Son, with Michael Harvey, 1970; descriptive leaflet for sundial, High Street, Biggar, 1970: 83, 85

Les Hirondelles, with Ron Costley, screenprint, 1970: 83

A Patch for a Rip-Tide Sail, with Margot Sandeman, screenprint, 1970: 55

Sheaves, folding card, screen print, 1970: 56, 61

A Use for Old Beehives, with Richard Demarco, folding card, 1970: 94

Boats of Letters, Tarasque Press,1970

Xmas Rose, with John Furnival, Christmas card, 1970: 105

Zulu Chieftain, with A. Doyle Moore (American typographer), screen print, 1971

A Sea Street Anthology, photograph by Gloria Wilson, 1971

Homage to Donald McGill, 1971: 120, 139

Flags, with acknowledgements to Simon Cutts, 1971

The Sign of the Nudge, with Michael Harvey, 1971: 116

The Harbour, photograph by Diane Tammes, 1971: 116

The Old Nobby, photograph by Diane Tammes, 1971: 146

Sails/Waves 1, Design for wall ceramic, with Ron Costley, screen print, 1971: 155–6

Sails/Waves 2, with Ron Costley, screen print, 1971

I Saw Three Ships, with Ron Costley, screen print, 1971

A Heart-Shape, with Ron Costley, 1971, screen print, 1971: 102

Birch-Bark, photograph by Diane Tammes, 1971

The Land's Shadows, with Michael Harvey, 1971, Christmas Card for Daedalus Press: 174

Kite: Willing Wings, photograph by Diane Tammes, New Year folding card, 1971

Tree Shells, with Ian Gardner, 1971: 128, 146

Catches, with Margot Sandeman, screen print, 1971[2]

Unicorn, I. H. Finlay yacht-model, photograph by Diane Tammes, folding card, 1971

Elegy for Whimbrel and Petrel, with Ian Gardner, Sepia Press, 1971

Xmas Morn, with Michael Harvey, Christmas Card, 1971: 174

V. Poem/Prints

Poem/Print No. 11 ('Xmas Star'), with John Furnival, screen print, 1969: 26, 43

Seams, screen print, 1969: 60

Evening/Sail 2, screen print, 1971: 146

Errata, with David Button, two prints in folder, 1970: 64–5, 72

Catameringue, with Peter Grant, screen print, 1970: 60

2. Sandeman's drawing is of a chestnut leaf, with chestnut 'conkers' on strings. Finlay's message in the card sent to me reads: 'Love from Ian 'Beaten but Unconkered' October 1971'.

Poem/print no. 14 ('Xmas Rose'), with John Furnival, 1970: 35, 60

The Little Seamstress, with Richard Demarco, screen print, 1970: 63, 68–9, 175

Homage to Mozart, with Ron Costley, screen print, 1970: 94, 143, 156

Scottish Zulu, with David Button, screen print, 1970: 63, 94, 98

Archangel, with Sydney McK. Glen, lithograph in folder, Christmas 1970: 106

Seven plates from Edgar J. March's 'Sailing Drifters', printed for Ceolfrith Press, Sunderland, folding print, 1970

A Rock Rose, with Richard Demarco, screen print, 1970: 175

Glossary, with Richard Demarco, print in folder, 1971: 64, 72

Seashells, with Ian Proctor, print in folder, 1971: 131–3, 135, 174

The Little Drummer Boy, with Ron Costley, screen print, 1971

Homage to Vuillard, with Michael Harvey, screen print, 1971: 131, 148, 151

Prinz Eugen (homage to gomringer), with Ron Costley, 1971: 143, 166–7

Shenval Christmas Poem Print ('The Flower of the Fal'), with Ron Costley, folding print, 1971: 175, 178

WORKS BY STEPHEN BANN

With references to the correspondence

I. Books and editions

Experimental Painting: Construction, Abstraction, Destruction, Reduction, London: Studio Vista, 1970: 56, 59, 60, 65, 69

(Ed.) Special number on 'Structuralism', *20th Century Studies*, 3, May 1970: 36, 61

(Ed.) Special number on 'Directions in the nouveau roman', *20th Century Studies*, 6, December 1971: 123–4, 162–3

(Ed.) *The Tradition of Constructivism*, Documents of Modern Art, New York: Viking Press, 1974: 37, 39, 44, 56, 118

II. Critical texts, commentaries and articles

'Ian Hamilton Finlay: Engineer and Bricoleur', booklet included in folder *Ceolfrith* 5, Ceolfrith Press, Bookshop Gallery, Sunderland, 1970: 91–2

'Land/Sea Indoor sundial': text included with edition of small sundials by Ian Hamilton Finlay, 1970: 47–49

'The Biggar Sundial', leaflet on sundial installed in High Street, Biggar, September 1970: 83

Seashells: text included in poem folder, with Ian Proctor and Ron Costley, 1970: 132–3, 135

Afterword to Ian Hamilton Finlay, *Honey by the Water*, Los Angeles: Black Sparrow Press, 1973: 75–6, 78, 82, 94–5, 107, 118

'Bernard Lassus: Ambiance', *Art and Artists*, June 1971, pp. 20–23: 113

Text for exhibition of Neon Poems, Richard Demarco Gallery, Edinburgh, December 1971: 154–5, 160, 171

Introduction to Systems Group exhibition catalogue, Whitechapel Gallery, London, Arts Council of Great Britain, 8 March–9 April 1972 (and touring to other galleries throughout the UK): 159

'L'anti-histoire de Henry Esmond', *Poétique*, 9, 1972, pp. 61–79: 94, 140, 181

Ian Hamilton Finlay: An Illustrated Essay, with a bibliography and catalogue of works exhibited at the Scottish National Gallery of Modern Art (6 July –6 August 1972), The MacRobert Centre, University of Stirling (9 October –1 November 1972), The Laing Art Gallery, Newcastle (11 November–9 December 1972): 168–9, 173, 182–86

III. Poems

'Amber Sands', poem construction, Brighton Festival, 1967: 25–6, 27

'Field, after Francis Ponge', poem booklet, Tarasque Press, 1972: 37

'Landscape of St Ives, Huntingdonshire', poem card, Tarasque Press, 1970: 44

'Vierzehnheiligen (the) (three) (ovals) of Balthasar Neumann', poem card, Tarasque Press, 1971: 120, 135–6, 164–5

'The Garden as a parenthesis', poem card, Tarasque Press, 1971: 135–7, 164–5

'Doves over the Sarthe at Solesmes', poem card, Tarasque Press, 1971: 141

BIOGRAPHICAL INDEX

Agam, Yaacov (Israeli kinetic artist, b. 1928), 140
Albers, Josef (German-born artist, 1888–1967), 140
Allan, Maxwell (Scottish letter carver and sculptor), 30, 31, 52, 63, 76, 79–80
Almansi, Guido (Italian writer and editor, 1931–2001), 18, 61, 124, 162, 164, 166
Amaya, Mario (American editor and art critic, 1933–86), 46
Apollinaire, Guillaume (French poet, 1880–1918), 46
Armstrong, Michael (English collector), 167

Bacon, Francis (English painter, 1909–92), 176
Baljeu, Joost (Dutch constructivist artist, 1925–91), 113
Barthes, Roland (French writer and theorist, 1915–80), 94
Botticelli, Sandro (Italian Renaissance painter, c. 1445–1510), 133
Boudin, Eugène (French painter, 1824–98), 125, 127
Bowler, Berjouhi (English editor and artist), 56
Brandon, Ruth (English writer, b. 1943), 88
Burns, Robert (Scottish poet, 1759–96), 89
Butler, Lawrence (English playwright), 118
Butor, Michel (French writer, b. 1926), 18, 124, 130, 140

Cage, John (American composer, 1912–92)), 62
Cameron, Julia Margaret (English photographer, 1817–81), 146
Carlyle, Thomas (Scottish writer, 1795–1881), 169
Carrell, Christopher (English art gallery director and editor), 98, 104, 107, 119–20, 122–3, 126, 134, 136, 139, 140, 143, 169, 173, 174
Chopin, Henri (French poet and editor, 1922–2008), 156
Clark, Lord [Kenneth] (English art historian and broadcaster, 1903–83), 128
Clark, Thomas A. (Scottish poet, b. 1944), 17
Clarke, Austin (Irish poet and playwright, 1896–1974), 76, 151
Cobbing, Bob (English soundtext poet, 1920–2002), 104
Connolly, Cyril (English writer and critic, 1903–74), 114-5
Cooney, Seamus (American small press publisher), 95, 96–7, 98, 119

Cosmann, Milein (friend of Sidney Keyes), 114–5
Costley, Ron (English letter designer, book designer and Finlay collaborator, 1940–2015), 18, 61, 64, 85, 132, 133, 155
Creeley, Robert (American poet, 1926–2005), 35
Cutts, Simon (English poet, artist and small press publisher, b. 1943), 19, 20, 55, 61, 64, 67, 75, 81, 85, 89, 91, 103, 125, 145, 148–9, 150, 171–3

Dallier [Popper], Aline (French singer and academic), 62, 148
Daudet, Alphonse (French writer, 1840–97), 120
David, Jacques-Louis (French painter, 1748–1825), 32
Deighton, Elizabeth (English editor), 26, 29
Delacroix, Eugène (French painter, 1798–1863), 102
Denis, Maurice (French painter, 1870–1943), 69, 89, 90, 93, 128
Demarco, Hugo (Argentine-born French kinetic artist, 1932–95), 57
Dorfles, Gillo (Italian critic, b. 1910), 69
Demarco, Richard (Scottish art gallery director and artist, b. 1930), 54, 58, 63, 151, 154, 171, 179, 180
Democritus (Greek Pre-Socratic philosopher), 119
Eccles, Viscount [David] (Conservative politician and Minister for the Arts, 1904–99), 84, 86, 121, 126, 150
Ede, H. S. [Jim] (English art collector, 1895–1990), 26, 29, 43, 57, 59, 61

Fargue, Léon-Paul (French poet, 1876–1947), 62, 70
Fernbach-Flarsheim, Carl (Polish-born American poet, b. 1921), 136, 138
Finlay [Swan], Susan [Sue] (wife of Ian Hamilton Finlay, b. 1943), 28, 32, 40, 57, 75, 91, 94, 127, 153
Foucault, Michel (French historian and philosopher, 1926–84), 78–9
Furnival, John (English artist and small press publisher, b. 1933), 25, 48, 52, 106, 169
Fuseli, Henry (Swiss-born English painter, 1741–1825), 106

Gabo, Naum (Russian constructivist sculptor, 1890–1977), 118, 120, 125
Gadney, Reg (English writer and painter, b. 1941), 175, 178
Gardner, Ian (English painter and Finlay collaborator, b. 1944), 20, 85, 128, 154, 163, 165
Gauguin, Paul (French painter, 1848–1903), 69
Gill, Eric (English letter cutter, sculptor and typographer, 1882–1940), 81

Gillis, Astrid (Scottish poet and friend of the Finlays), 46
Ginsberg, Allen (American poet, 1926–97), 35
Glen, Duncan (Scottish editor, 1933–2008), 85, 88–9, 90, 95
Glen, Michael [Hamish] (Scottish printer, b. 1941), 92
Gomringer, Eugen (Bolivian-born German poet, b. 1925), 66, 155, 166, 183
Goodman, Lord [Arnold] (English lawyer and Chairman of Arts Council, 1915–95), 86, 121, 124, 126, 150
Gosling, Nigel (English art and dance critic, 1909–82), 64, 65
Greenaway, Kate (English artist, 1846–1901), 128
Greenwood, Nigel (British art dealer, 1941–2004), 45
Grimond, Lord [Jo] (Scottish Liberal politician, 1913–93), 168, 180
Grist, Anthony (English poet and cleric, b. 1951), 137, 146, 148, 149, 152, 153, 156, 159, 161, 164, 168, 182
Gunn, Ronald (Scottish photographer, d. 2013), 28, 29, 36

Hall, Douglas (Director of Scottish National Gallery of Modern Art), 20, 86, 178, 182
Hall, Viscount [George] (Post Office Chairman, 1913–85), 103
Hart, Judith (Scottish politician, 1924–91), 150
Harvey, Michael (British lettering designer, letter carver and Finlay collaborator, 1931–2013), 79, 81, 82, 84–5, 87, 133, 137, 143, 150, 152, 154, 157–8, 160, 162–3, 165–6, 167–8, 171–2, 177, 180
Hawkins, Oliver (English designer and teacher, b. 1944), 34, 140
Henderson, William (English architect), 152, 163, 180
Higgins, Dick (Anglo-American editor, poet and artist, 1938–98), 81, 119
Hill, Anthony (English constructivist artist, b. 1930), 61
Hincks, Gary (English artist and Finlay collaborator), 16
Hockney, David (English artist, b. 1937), 64
Houédard, Dom Sylvester (English poet and ecumenical writer, 1924–92), 104
Hulten, Pontus (Swedish gallery director, 1924–2006), 152
Huxley, Aldous (English writer, 1894–1963), 35
Hyams, Edward (English garden historian and journalist, 1910–75), 16, 72, 107, 113

Irwin, Gwyther (English artist, 1931–2008), 180

Jackson, Thomas [Tom], (English union official, 1925–2003), 119
James, Henry (Anglo-American novelist, 1843–1916), 106
Jandl, Ernst (Austrian poet, 1925–2000), 31, 34, 144

Jekyll, Gertrude (English garden designer, 1843–1932), 129

Karpel, Bernard (American art librarian and bibliographer, 1911–86), 20, 36, 39, 44, 46, 53, 57, 68, 70–1, 73, 74, 79, 99, 107, 122, 124, 128, 134, 136, 138, 140, 144, 161

Kenedy, Robert (Anglo-Hungarian poet and librarian, d. 1980), 64, 88, 90, 97, 99, 139, 179, 182

Keyes, Sidney (English poet, 1922–43), 106, 113–14

Kipling, Rudyard (English writer, 1865–1936), 19, 21, 146, 151, 176, 181

Kristeva, Julia (Bulgarian-born French writer and academic, b. 1941), 95

Kriwet, Ferdinand (German artist, b. 1942), 71

Larionov, Mikhail (Russian painter, 1881–1964), 91

Lassus, Bernard (French artist and garden designer, b. 1929), 100, 102, 113, 136, 181

Lauder, Sir Harry (Scottish singer, 1870–1950), 62

Laughlin, James (American poet and publisher, 1914–97), 54

Lévi-Strauss, Claude (French anthropologist, 1908–2009), 18, 69, 92, 93

Lindsay, Maurice (Scottish poet and broadcaster, 1918–2009), 90

Lucie-Smith, Edward (English writer, poet and art critic, b. 1933), 28

Lutyens, Sir Edwin (English architect, 1869–1944), 129

MacDiarmid, Hugh (Scottish poet, 1892–1978), 65, 79, 81

McGill, Donald (English postcard designer, 1875–1962), 120, 139

Mackintosh, Charles Rennie (Scottish architect and designer,1868–1928), 186

Malina, Frank (American kinetic artist and journal editor, 1912–81), 69, 70

Mallarmé, Stéphane (French poet, 1842–98), 66, 149

Manduca, John Borg (Maltese architect, b. 1934), 26

Marinetti, Filippo (Italian Futurist poet and journalist, 1876–1944), 142

Martin, J. H. (Editor of *Ships Monthly*), 35

Martin, James (Scottish Art College principal), 27

Martin, Kenneth (English painter and sculptor, 1905–84), 37, 44

Marx, Karl (German political philosopher, 1818–83), 37

Matisse, Henri (French painter, 1869–1954), 61

Mayer, Hansjörg (German typographer and publisher, b. 1943), 40, 57

Mayor, David (English editor and poet), 43

Medalla, David (Filipino-born kinetic artist, b. 1942), 29

Merchant, Moelwyn (Welsh academic, poet and priest, 1913–97), 75

Mills, Stuart (English poet, artist and small press publisher, 1940–2006), 20, 30, 37, 40, 45, 48, 63, 91, 96, 125, 127, 137, 154, 163, 172–3, 174–5

Mon, Franz (German artist, b. 1926), 71

Montgomery, Stuart (British poet, founder and publisher of Fulcrum Press, b. 1940), 35, 42, 53, 65, 86

Morgan, Edwin [Yeddie] (Scottish poet, 1920–2019), 144

Morris, Robert (American artist, b. 1931), 62

Morris, William (English designer, artist and writer, 1834–96), 129

Motherwell, Robert (American painter, 1915–91), 44, 46, 53

Naughtie, James (Scottish broadcaster, b. 1951), 180

Neumann, Balthasar (German architect, 1687–1753), 120

Nye, Robert (English poet, b. 1939), 71

Oldenburg, Claes (American Pop sculptor, b. 1929), 175

Orwell [Brownell], Sonia (editorial assistant, widow of George Orwell, 1918–80), 114

Osborne, Charles (Australian-born Director of Literature, Arts Council, b. 1927), 144

Palmer, Samuel (English painter, 1805–81), 45

Panofsky, Erwin (German-born American art historian, 1892–1968), 16, 99, 104, 106

Paolozzi, Sir Eduardo (Scottish sculptor, 1929–2005), 140

Pater, Walter (English aesthetic writer and critic, 1839–94), 19, 99, 140, 142, 149

Pevsner, Nicholas (German-born English architectural historian, 1902–83), 120

Pinget, Robert (Swiss-born French writer, 1919–97), 57, 124, 163, 165

Ponge, Francis (French poet and essayist, 1899–1988), 82, 165

Popper, Frank (Czech-born French art historian, b. 1918), 136, 139, 140, 144, 181

Powell, Enoch (English Conservative politician, 1912–98), 63

Praz, Mario (Italian writer and critic, 1896–1982), 114

Proctor, Ian (English yacht designer, 1918–92), 77, 131, 132

Proust, Marcel (French writer, 1871–1922), 19, 50, 106

Reichardt, Jasia (Polish-born English art critic, editor and curator, b. 1933), 16

René, Denise (French art gallery director, 1913–2012), 68

Riefenstahl, Leni (German film director and actress, 1902–2003), 117

Roberts, John (Scottish photographer) 159

Rosenthal, M. L. (American academic, 1917–96), 21

Ross, Alan (British poet and editor, 1922–2001), 31

Rot [Roth], Dieter (Swiss artist, 1930–98), 40, 57

Rousseau, Jean-Jacques (French-Swiss writer, 1712–78), 93
Ruskin, John (English writer and artist, 1819–1900), 50

Sandeman, Margaret (Scottish painter and Finlay collaborator), 1922–2009), 92
Satie, Eric (French composer and pianist, 1866–1925), 62, 64
Schwitters, Kurt (German-born artist, 1887–1948), 50, 66
Scobie, Stephen (Scottish-born Canadian poet and critic), 89
Seurat, Georges (French painter, 1859–91), 128
Sévigné, Marquise [Marie] de (French letter writer, 1626–96), 78
Sharkey, John (British poet and editor, b. 1936), 104
Sheeler [McGuffie], Jessie (Scottish friend of the Finlays, co-founder of Wild Hawthorn Press, b. 1938), 127
Sollers, Philippe (French writer and journal editor, b. 1936), 95, 96
Solt, Mary Ellen (American poet and academic, 1920–2007) , 134
Spender, Stephen (English poet, 1909–95), 114
Spengler, Oswald (German historian, 1880–1936), 38
Stanford, Derek (English writer and friend of Finlay, 1918–2008), 59, 153
Steadman, Philip (British academic, editor and typographer, b. 1942), 88
Stein, Gertrude (American writer, 1874–1946), 91
Stevenson, Robert Louis (Scottish poet and writer, 1850–94), 140, 176
Styles, James (English photographer), 8, 28
Suenens, Cardinal [Leo Jozef] (Archbishop of Malines, 1904–96), 95, 96
Summerfield, Geoffrey (English academic and editor, 1931–91), 39, 46

Tammes, Diane (Scottish photographer), 36, 116, 164, 166
Tatlin, Vladimir (Russian constructivist artist, 1885–1953), 125
Thackeray, William Makepeace (English novelist, 1811–63), 82, 94, 181
Thomas, Dylan (Welsh poet, 1914–53), 126
Thorpe, John (English wood carver and Finlay collaborator), 42, 105, 146
Tinguely, Jean (Swiss kinetic artist, 1925–91), 134, 159
Todd, Ruthven (Scottish poet, 1914–78), 114–5
Tweedsmuir, Lady [Susan] (Scottish politician, 1882–1977), 79, 84

Vasarely, Victor (Hungarian-born French kinetic artist, 1906–97), 68

Wales, Prince of [Charles] (British heir to the throne, b. 1948), 57, 59
Wallis, Alfred (English artist, 1855–1942), 29, 43, 59
Watteau, Antoine (French painter, 1684–1721), 52, 128
Weaver, Mike (English academic, critic and historian of photography, b. 1937), 8, 75
Webster, John (English Jacobean playwright, c. 1580–1634), 106
Wheatley, Andres (French singer), 62
White, Eric Walter (Director of Literature, Arts Council, 1905–85), 84, 86, 105, 121
Wilde, Oscar (Irish writer, 1854–1900), 18, 92, 93
Willett, John (English writer, translator and journalist, 1917–2002), 40, 57, 138
Williams, Jonathan (American poet, publisher, essayist and photographer, 1929–2008), 17, 21, 144, 169–70, 182, 186
Williams, Terence (American rare book librarian, University of Kansas), 45
Wright, Edward (British typographer, designer, artist and writer, 1912–88), 144
Wright, Robin (English publisher), 68
Wynter, Bryan (English painter, 1915–75), 114–15

Zavriew, André (French diplomat and writer), 95
Zurbrugg, Nicholas (English poet, editor and academic, 1947–2001), 156
Zwemmer, Anton (Dutch-born bookshop proprietor, 1907–95), 115